07

Work experience in secondary schools

Routledge Education Books

Advisory editor: John Eggleston
Professor of Education
University of Keele

Work experience in secondary schools

John Eggleston
Professor of Education
University of Keele

Routledge & Kegan Paul
London, Boston, Melbourne and Henley

First published in 1982
by Routledge & Kegan Paul Ltd
39 Store Street, London WC1E 7DD,
9 Park Street, Boston, Mass. 02108, USA,
296 Beaconsfield Parade, Middle Park,
Melbourne, 3206, Australia, and
Broadway House, Newtown Road,
Henley-on-Thames, Oxon RG9 1EN
Set in IBM Press Roman by Columns, Reading
and printed in Great Britain by
T.J. Press (Padstow) Ltd,
Padstow, Cornwall
Editorial selection, Introduction and
Chapter 1 © John Eggleston 1982

Library of Congress Cataloging in Publication Data

Work experience in secondary schools.

(Routledge education books)
Includes index.
1. Education, Cooperative – Case studies. I. Eggleston,
John. II. Series.
LB1029.C6W625 1982   373.2'7   82-11298

ISBN 0-7100-9219-9

Contents

Contributors

Brenda Hall is a Careers Tutor at Netherhall School in Cambridge.

Roger Davies is Director of Studies at Comberton Village College, Cambridge.

Helen Parry is Assistant Careers Tutor at Long Road Sixth Form College, Cambridge.

John Harris is Principal of Newpark Comprehensive School in Blackrock, Co. Dublin.

Margo Gunn is a Project Leader at the Bayswater Centre, Bristol.

Alastair Moir is a Project Leader at the Bayswater Centre, Bristol.

Roger White is a Project Leader at the Bayswater Centre, Bristol

Mervyn H. Douglas was formerly a member of the staff of Orangefield Secondary School, Belfast.

E.T. Naughton is Head of Chemistry/Science at Ynysawdre Comprehensive School, Bridgend.

B.D. Hannaford is Principal of Marion High School, Colvelly Park, South Australia.

Nigel Grant is Head of the Department of Education, University of Glasgow.

Introduction

Work experience schemes are becoming a key component of the curriculum of secondary schooling throughout the Western world. Fundamental changes in the nature of work, as well as the change in the distribution and availability of work for young school leavers is turning an infrequently provided experience into a central provision in many secondary schools. A wide range of schemes have been developed, including work study, simulation, link courses, pairing and many others.

This volume presents nine studies of a variety of forms of development in schools. Each shows not only the development of work experience activities, but also the staffing and administrative implications that arise.

There are accounts of school-based developments at Netherhall and Comberton Schools and Long Road Sixth Form College, Cambridge; Newpark School, Dublin; The Bayswater Centre, Bristol; Orangefield School, Belfast; Ynysawdre Comprehensive School, Bridgend; and Marion High School, South Australia. There is also a report of activity in the USSR and Eastern Europe. Yet there are many unresolved ideological, social and economic issues underlying the development of work experience and these are considered in an extended editorial introduction.

The authors of the case studies join me in expressing our appreciation of the many colleagues in and around our institutions who have co-operated in the developments reported and also in the reporting of them. Writing about work experience is in itself an intensive collaborative experience of work. Our thanks also go to Kathleen McKeown for assembling and typing the manuscript, to the Keele Education Library for consistent help in providing and checking source material, and to David Godwin of Routledge & Kegan Paul for his encouragement of the project.

John Eggleston

Chapter 1

Work experience and schooling

John Eggleston

Most subjects have been added to the school curriculum only when informal education by family, church or community becomes unable to ensure the learning needed for adult roles. The history of the '3 Rs', school science, physical education, environmental studies and sex education show that all these subjects have 'arrived' in this way. Vocational education and industrial training became part of the curriculum in areas where pre-occupational training was unavailable informally. Work itself, the newest subject in the curriculum, has a similar history — though recent demographic and economic events across the world have speeded the historical process.

In the recent past the experience of work was indivisible from the experience of family, community and society. It is only during the past century and a half that work, for most citizens, has been taken apart from the day-to-day life of family and community and transferred to separate institutions — factories, shops, offices, workshops and warehouses. Such institutions are increasingly 'closed': for reasons of complex technology, security, privacy, hygiene or hazard they are only accessible to those who work therein and within their prescribed working hours.

Yet the twentieth century has seen a further development in the nature of the experience of work. Not only is it a separable part of human experience, but it is also one that is not being made available to all human beings. When twentieth century societies first experienced mass unemployment it was believed that this was but a temporary phenomenon caused by short-term 'malfunctionings' of the economic mechanism such as depression or recession. Now it is realised that unless effective alternative strategies are identified and adopted, such 'malfunctioning' may become a permanent feature: unemployment become structural.

Young people and work

In this new situation major problems arise for young people. By far the majority are beyond the reach of any school 'remedy' and it is misleading and dangerous to imply otherwise. But some have considerable relevance for the work of schools. One is that in many countries unemployment, especially for the young, co-exists with unfilled vacancies in many of the areas of work which require skills, understandings and attributes not generally possessed by school leavers. Thus there are shortages of young people for vacancies in the 'servicing trades' responsible for the maintenance of motor cars, television sets and other domestic appliances, building maintenance and even gardening and window cleaning. There are also recurring shortages of candidates for higher level work in computing, electronics and a range of scientific and creative occupations. Of course, not all of these shortages are 'real', some are 'technical', but there is little doubt that many do exist.

A second problem is that young people who leave school and do not experience work seem to find it increasingly difficult to obtain it. Potential employers believe that some kind of atrophy develops; just as the muscles in a broken leg lose their power, so a total lack of work experience is believed to diminish the capacity to satisfy the very requirements of work such as industry, responsibility and punctuality.

A third, and perhaps the most fundamental, problem is closely associated with the second; it is that work experience provides the basic contexts for 'normal' life. These include the use of time, the achievement of social 'standing' with its rights and duties and many of the attitudes and values that underpin participation in all the other human contexts offered by society. We may express the situation in two ways. One is that vocational identity is the key to social identity. The other is that work is the central instrument of social control in modern societies. Without the experience of work, how can the individual develop an adequate social identity and how can the society exercise the social control over its members necessary to achieve stability and continuity?

The experience of work

We have now come to the crucial nature of work experience. Like most human experiences, it has been taken for granted while its existence seemed assured. We have come to see its importance more clearly when its availability is at risk. It is necessary to notice, however, that work experience involves a dual context. One is the context of the specific job being done – with its skills, expectations, norms and values. The other is the context of the labour market with its organisations of labour and management, its norms of production, payment and security. Both aspects will be examined in the consideration of work experience provided by the schools.

Almost all young people see work as the key to the achievement of full masculinity or femininity. Willis's study of working-class boys in an English comprehensive school in an inner-city area depicts the social pressures on the boys to take their place on the shop floor and so earn the acceptance of the community to which they belong (1978). These boys need to prove themselves amongst their work-mates as capable of facing and surviving the realities of the factory floor with its 'hard and brutalising' conditions.

Willis writes:

> The lads are not choosing careers or particular jobs, they are com- mitting themselves to a future of generalised labour. Most work — or the 'grafting' they accept they will face — is equilibrated by the overwhelming need for instant money, the assumption that all work is unpleasant and that what really matters is the potential particular work situations hold for self and particularly masculine expression, diversions and 'laffs' as learnt creatively in the counter-school culture. These things are quite separate from the intrinsic nature of any task. This view does not contradict, for the moment, the over- whelming feeling that work is something to look forward to . . . the lure of the prospect of money and cultural membership amongst 'real men' beckons very seductively as refracted through their own culture.

But as the 'lads'' attitudes clearly show, of even greater importance than specific occupational role is the set of understandings and the self-image that the individual brings to his roles. This *identity* with which the individual imbues his roles is crucial to the way he plays them, modifies them and develops them, and to his own personal future within them. A label, such as lathe operator, is but an incomplete guide to human behaviour in work — the identity with which the incumbent fills the role is the key component. How does he perceive himself as a lathe operator? He has chosen the work or is it a forced decision? If the former, what are his alternatives? Are they realistic or only based on fantasy? How does he adjust to the role in the absence of alternatives? What are the implications for his other social behaviour? Fundament- ally, is the vocational identity, with all its consequences, compatible with his ego and his self-image? If it is not, how may greater compati- bility develop within the role?

The development of vocational identities is complex in modern society. In early, labour-intensive industrialisation, when large numbers of workers were required to perform routine and repetitive tasks, individual identity seldom came to exercise a dominant influence on production. Their self-image was of relatively little consequence to most employers. Young people were fitted into their roles in conditions which Durkheim described as 'mechanical solidarity'; the role transcendent, the individual subordinate.

The concept of identity alerts us to an alternative process. It is one in which young people may prefer to 'contract in' to both the specific job and the labour market generally rather than to accept them passively. This new approach is highly relevant to some aspects of contemporary social conditions. It is compatible with the expressed views of young people who wish to 'count for something' in society rather than to be 'on the receiving end' of 'the system'. But it is also appropriate for the needs of some sectors of modern industry which calls for human beings not to act as 'machines', but to use their capacity to adapt, adjust and initiate. For such occupational roles an active vocational identity rather than a passive vocational role is highly preferable.

Unless an acceptable vocational identity can be achieved, then life for the individual is likely to be at best incomplete or compartmentalised; at worst, frustrating, enervating and incompatible. Problems are likely to arise not only for the individual, but also for society — which is likely to experience widespread alienation or disruptive behaviour if vocational identities are generally felt to be unsatisfactory. And if work is not available the problems are likely to occur in an even more serious form.

The achievement of work identity

We have already noted that, until recently, most vocational identities were acquired by predominantly informal means. The learning of occupational roles literally began in the cradle as the child saw his parents at work in homes, farms and workshops. The phrase 'like father like son' epitomised not only the informality of learning but also the predictability of the vocational role that awaited most young people. The circumstances of the parents determined the future role of the young and the learning appropriate to it. Such identities were strongly reinforced by the norms of the community which defined, often with great precision, such things as man's work and woman's work; noble work and base work. Definitions of this kind were sometimes strongly reinforced by initiation ceremonies as a prelude to entry to adult vocational roles and still feature in some apprenticeship schemes.

Informal mechanisms for achieving vocational identities are, however, not always appropriate in modern dynamic societies, where occupational structures are changing rapidly and in which it may be possible for young people to have sufficient knowledge of the available roles in sufficient time to learn them and identify with them in anticipation. A characteristic problem of all advanced industrial societies is the rapid growth of new occupational groups such as electronics engineers, motor car repairers and salesmen, advertising and sales personnel, which has meant that many young people enter work to undertake roles for which they have been able to achieve little or no preliminary identification. New generations of vocational identity may commence with each new initiative in technology and commerce.

School and vocational identity

Schools have usually played only a small part in helping young people to achieve vocational identity. Though in the past half-century they have come to exercise a major role in helping to identify talent through the examination and accreditation systems, there has been little attempt to assist the young in achieving the identities to accompany the examination qualifications. There has been even less success in helping those without examination qualifications to achieve such identities. This has led to many problems. Not only have many young people lacked an adequate identity for work, but also, for many, for the other aspects of life that are linked to work. There has, for example, been remarkably little preparation for such activities as leadership in the workers' unions — roles that undeniably play a central part in modern societies. As a result, there are major problems in identifying leaders for these bodies at both local and regional level with important consequences for the day-to-day running of our occupational and economic systems. Political and community identities also have seldom received the attention they deserve; potential leaders here too are often in short supply.

An important element in vocational identity has commonly been the social background of the young. Many writers have drawn attention to the small part played by schools in orienting and preparing young people for work. Becker (1963) has suggested that school makes little impact other than to offer legitimation of the differences brought about by home and community. As Willis (1978) says: 'The difficult thing to explain about how middle class kids get middle class jobs is why others let them. The difficult thing to explain about how working class kids get working class jobs is why they let themselves.'

Bourdieu (1972) sees this to be a consequence of dominance of social and cultural reproduction processes that schools reinforce but do not change. Many writers, such as Lazerson (1971) and Bowles and

7

Gintis (1976), have come to see the growing potential importance of school as a transition institution into the labour force; an institution which 'accredits' young people with the various needs of the labour market (including unemployment) and achieves the necessary correspondence between supply and demand. Grubb and Lazerson (1981) demonstrate ways in which even new strategies of career education have, in practice, been used to stratify the school system, and to separate lower-class and ethnic minority youth from their white and middle-class peers.

Providing work experience in the schools

Yet despite the difficulties, the present-day economic and social systems compel schools to take an active role in the achievement of work identity and the provision of experience in which it may occur. Watts (1981) writes:

> The world of work is central to our society, and to the generation and distribution of wealth within it. For schools to neglect the world of work behind rhetoric like 'concern for the whole person' — as though the role of worker was not an important *part* of the whole person — is abjectly to neglect a critical part of their educational responsibilities. . . . The need for schools to address the world of work, but to do so in a critical and dynamic way, is all the more important because of the crisis that is taking place in relation to the place of work in our society.

The new planned work experience schemes in schools take many forms. Essentially, they are interventionist strategies designed to provide a substitute experience of work when the 'normal' social forces fail to deliver 'the real thing'. Work experience is, of course, a long way from the real thing: it can offer work tasks in work environments, but it cannot offer normal pay and tenure — essential adjuncts to identity as a worker.

There have always been some educators who have believed that work experience is too important to leave to chance — or just to be talked about in the schools. J.S. Mill, J. Dewey and Kurt Hahn advocated this view strongly and in different ways it is embodied in the curricula of the German Technical High Schools and the Soviet Young Pioneers. But in present conditions, when work experience cannot be relied upon 'just to happen' for the majority of young people, its provision becomes an urgent social need. In some countries it has become a major focus of national politics. Australia provides a typical example. In November 1979 the Commonwealth and States announced a series of initiatives known as the School-to-Work Transition Programme. $259 million are being spent over the next five years on a range of technical courses, student counselling and special programmes for young people. The reason for the government's action was obvious. Already one young Australian in five was out of work, and another 50,000 were due to enter the labour market with little or no hope of a job.

In Australia − as in the United States, Denmark, Britain and almost every other developed country, inevitably the issues are polarised in political debate. On the one hand, there is enthusiasm for 'educational solutions' − to offer the opportunity for the young to acquire more fully the skill, knowledge, attitudes and perceptions along with as much as possible of the experience needed to constitute a vocational identity. On the other hand, there is the view that creation of more jobs is the only worthwhile objective; if this is done adequately the rest can once again be left to chance.* The contributors to this volume are largely, but not solely, concerned with examining the former position. At its fullest considerations the latter, involving changes in the total structure of societies, often of a radical nature, is beyond the scope of the schools. But it may be argued that many of the 'educational' solutions, far from being palliative, have the capacity to create jobs within existing societies and a number of schools are already involved in putting this capacity into practice.

Variations between practice in schools are widespread as befits a developing field. The categorisation of process is presented in some detail in the forthcoming pages. The categories used are:

Infusion
Work experience courses
Work creation schemes
Link courses
Work simulation schemes.

Infusion

We may begin with one of the oldest forms of work experience − that in which it is *infused* into the total curriculum rather than constituting

*Similar debate surrounds the extensive operations of the British Manpower Services Commission with its Youth Opportunity Programmes and Job Creation Schemes, now being made available to all young unemployed persons, described by Holland of the Manpower Services Commission as 'the prototype of a new kind of education for all of Britain's school leavers'. Such schemes and all others for post school leavers, though of crucial importance for the schools, are beyond the scope of this volume on initiatives in the school.

a separate *additional* activity. Only recently has this total approach been labelled as infusion — a term now widely used in the United States. Yet for centuries schools have provided work experience exactly relevant for the needs of their elite students — those who are entering the learned and academic professions. Such students have experienced working in the academic library, acting as teachers with titles such as monitor or prefect, conducting religious worship and much else. Alas, such work experience has offered little to those who were not destined for academic, clerical, legal or library careers: schools have often been castigated for their concern for the future work of the few rather than the many. More recently, however, a conscious strategy of infusion has brought work experience into the whole curriculum for some students. Science has concerned itself with the practice of science in industry, mathematics with its commercial and business utilisation, linguistics with careers in communication at all levels. In particular, work in design, craft and technology has been closely linked with the experience of industrial production — indeed the subject area has gone under the title of Industrial Arts in many countries. In all these activities, visits to industry and from industrialists form an important feature. The argument for such infusions is that preparation for work is not just another subject — it is what school is all about.

A specific attempt to infuse work into the curriculum has been the Schools Council Industry Project. Jamieson and Lightfoot (1981), both members of the project team, note that:

> the most common way of including teaching about work was by incorporating the topic into a great course that already existed in the school for the fourth and/or fifth years. The majority of these courses are based round the theme of 'living in a modern industrial society'. Such courses are very often designed, or at least used, by schools to accommodate a variety of 'demands' made by those outside the school (for example, parents, industry, or the LEA) for the inclusion of subject matter which is thought to be necessary for a child's education, but which does not easily fit into an existing curriculum slot. Examples of these topics include health education, moral education, political education, economic education, occasionally careers education, and 'the world of work'.

But the authors are frank about the difficulties, however. They continue:

> One can immediately see the potential difficulties of such courses. The treatment of each issue area is likely to be relatively superficial because of the large amount of ground to be covered. The course is likely to lack conceptual coherence, particularly if it is taught by teachers from a variety of subject backgrounds, which is commonly the case.

They draw particular attention to the problem we have noticed already: that work experience tends to be offered more fully for precisely those children whose prospects in the labour market are most limited. In most secondary schools these are the 'non-examination' students. 'If there are omissions, then it is usually the top ability band which does not take the course, being left to concentrate on its examination courses.'

This is, of course, not essential, as Jamieson and Lightfoot recognise. But there are certainly difficulties.

The main source of the difficulty can be well illustrated by the case of pupil work experience, where the control of the experience which is to be examined passes out of the hands of the teacher. It is difficult to examine what pupils have learned about work from work experience placements which have all been markedly different from one another. Such problems can only be partly ameliorated by the use of a suitably designed Mode 3 CSE, where course-work makes an important contribution to the final results.

Though compellingly straightforward in principle, the practice of infusion is difficult. Quite apart from the problems of examinations, even when coherently planned as in the Schools Council Industry Project, the generations of tradition and academic teacher selection and training make it difficult for both schools and teachers to make the radical change across the board, whilst its very diffusion makes it difficult to evaluate. The objectives are easy to list, the achievements are distinctly harder to identify. Perhaps the way forward is to develop work experience as a well-established activity of the school system first and then to integrate it effectively in the whole curriculum. Certainly, the 'additive' arrangements which we now go on to describe seem, in the short run at least, to be able to offer more identifiable results.

Work experience courses

These are perhaps one of the best established of the 'additive' solutions within the schools. In such courses older pupils visit one or more vocational locations where they have the opportunity, over a period, to mix with workers at a variety of levels and to learn something of the formal and the informal culture of the work-place — the ways in which life is experienced by those who work therein. In some situations it is possible for pupils actually to experience work with its productive rhythms, its rewards and constraints, but unfortunately problems of union restrictions, insurance hazard and many other administrative difficulties generally restrict such opportunities to casual work and certain kinds of

11

agricultural situations. (Though in England and Wales some enabling legislation exists — such as the Education Work Experience Act of 1973.) Such courses are well-known, although some variations — such as 'shadowing' (where a pupil shadows an adult throughout his working day) — are less familiar. They fit happily into the contemporary orientation of many secondary schools where renewed emphases are being placed upon initiation into the life of the community. Such emphases have followed a recognition in that although children spend most of their life outside the school, they none the less have surprisingly few *entrées* into the adult world that exists beyond their homes and in the immediate neighbourhood. Whereas, in the past, children encountered working adults in many contexts and had many opportunities to identify with them, they may now seldom see a working adult other than the postman and the dustman. Work experience courses attempt to fill this dearth of first-hand experience.

Coles (1980) analyses work experience as follows:

> The broad ambit of work experience programmes is represented in the following diagram (Figure 1.2). This suggests that work experience involves two levels of activity. The first is somewhat narrow in focus, specifically relating to the student/job interface and involves the individual student's sampling and testing of vocational options. The second relates to work education as a curriculum development designed to enable students to prepare themselves for the world of work in all its aspects. These two aspects of work experience are necessarily interdependent. For example, even the

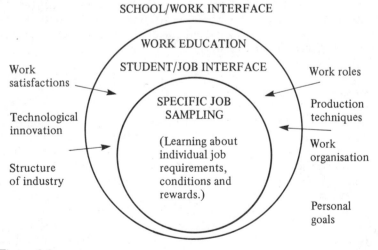

Figure 1.2

most narrowly defined scheme for student job testing will involve guiding assumptions about the broader work environment: the job expectations of specific student groups, what they require to be able to hold a job, the likelihood of relevance of possible changes in the work situation, etc. This level of activity in isolation cannot, however, present students with the opportunity to equip themselves to confront a rapidly changing work environment, and the growing uncertainties and complexities in the school and work interface.

The aims of work experience courses are well stated in the Department of Education and Science (England and Wales) Circular 7/74 of 1974. It states:

The principle which should underlie any work experience scheme is that pupils should be given an insight into the world of work, its disciplines and relationships. This principle, and the requirement of the Act that schemes for pupils of compulsory school age must form part of an educational programme, would not be satisfied by arrangements made whether in school or elsewhere, whose purpose was specifically or mainly to assess individuals for particular forms of employment, or to occupy pupils in producing articles for sale. Schemes should include provision within the school curriculum for preparation before the pupils take part in work experience and for following up and discussing the experience gained. Employers should be made fully aware of the aims of the scheme and should be invited to plan their part in co-operation with the schools.

Work experience should have value for pupils of varying ability and aptitudes and should neither be designed as vocational training nor aimed at a limited range of pupils only. If it is possible to arrange for a variety of types of work to be available the opportunity for drawing comparisons will obviously be increased. It would, however, be undesirable if the time spent by an individual pupil in any place of work were so short as to give only a superficial impression. The total amount of time spent out of school on work experience schemes, and its distribution, will necessarily vary according to local and individual circumstances. In deciding how much time is appropriate, schools and local authorities will need to take account of the time needed for supporting studies in school and to satisfy themselves that the total amount of time spent is appropriate within the educational programme of the pupils.

There are numerous examples of well-developed work experience courses in secondary schools. The arrangements made in some Cambridge schools are described in detail in the following chapters. Many schools have made such sophisticated and successful arrangements with local industry and provide placements of varying durations.

Some, but by no means all, are undertaken in connection with the Schools Council Industry Project. Some schools have their own well-documented reports of events, a typical example is *A Case Study in School-Industry Liaison*, available from Cheadle High School, North Staffordshire.

Many schools report a range of favourable outcomes from their work experience courses. A recurring one is that such courses establish links between industries and schools that did not exist before and that work opportunities previously unknown to the school become available to its pupils as a result. In some cases pupils are offered employment well before the completion of the course. There may, of course, be problems — a highly popular work experience course in a school may siphon off some of the pupils selected by the school for advanced courses in polytechnics or universities. For these and many other reasons, it is widely seen to be desirable to accompany work experience with appropriate guidance; the arrangement whereby guidance counsellors are linked to the pre-employment courses in the Irish schools (as Harris demonstrates in his chapter) is a good example of such strategies.

A typical example of work experience at various levels is that provided by the Swiss in most cantons. There work experience involves three stages (which may not exist in all schools and cantons):

1 visits to enterprises — usually of a few hours' duration to sample the ambience of the work place;
2 following student responses, extended conversations about work — in the workplace with experienced workers;
3 extended experiences in the workshop of 3-6 days.

This last is a relatively new scheme called *Schnupperlehre*, literally a 'sniff of learning' and is already available in the Cantons of Berne and Zurich. It appears likely to be adopted more widely in the near future. Notwithstanding their traditional appearance, these arrangements have a new and important role to play in Swiss affairs. Until recently, foreign guest-workers have performed most of the low status, 'dirty' jobs, allowing most Swiss to do higher status work. Since the economic recession, many guest-workers have been 'sent home', and their work is now being done by Swiss. A crucial task of the schools and guidance services is to make such work more 'acceptable' to the young; the *Schnupperlehre* plays an important role in this. A further emergent role of the *Schnupperlehre* appears to be to provide an opportunity for employers to select prospective employees; in addition to giving the young 'a sniff of work' it gives the employers a sniff of the young. One of the consequences of such a scheme is, inevitably, that it offers participants an 'early start' in job-selection, which may thereby disadvantage non-participants.

Similar strategies are adopted by the Austrian authorities in the 'Give it a try' one-week apprenticeships reported in *Vocational Training* (1977). In Denmark a range of work experience arrangements have developed. One is the Rodovre school — a little 'town' of buildings which are common in normal life. There is a bank, shops, a church, etc. Pupils in the last year of compulsory school can work in this 'town'. Among other subjects the following are offered in the 'Youth Town' courses: an introduction to economics in the banking and insurance rooms, personal and family finances in the savings bank house, communication in the post office, and a basic introduction to electronic data processing. Furthermore, there are courses introducing the young people to 'co-operation in school and on the job' in the town hall. When the theatre hall has been finished a programme introducing the young people to cultural activities will be established.

The daily work is carried out in close contact with trade representatives and educationalists in that any teaching that takes place in the 'Youth Town' is done by specialists placed at their disposal by institutions of further education and the trades. The plans, methods and suitable materials within each house are made by the teachers of the Innovative Centre and the individual experts. A continual revision of the courses is undertaken by representatives of the trades and teachers.

Work creation schemes

Closely linked with the provision of work experience — and a logical extension from it — is the creation or identification of work not currently being undertaken by existing paid labour. Here the school is not only able to provide work experience, but also to provide necessary services for the community. The report of the CERES project in Brunswick, Melbourne describes an urban environment field station project involving the reconstitution of ten acres of degraded urban land with community gardens, city farm, environmental displays, low energy building, low energy display and a community meeting place for community use and community support, public environmental education and training, school and tertiary projects, energy research and development, educational recreation and developing employment opportunities. The genesis of the project lay in the liaison of the seven local secondary schools in a joint body, the Brunswick Secondary Education Council (BRUSEC) and its work with a range of statutory and voluntary bodies. A detailed record of the project is available (Coles, 1979).

A notable work creation scheme at a school is the Study Work Programme at Marion High School, South Australia, the subject of a subsequent chapter. Here young people beyond minimum school leaving age work in an industrial setting within the school grounds. Working a thirty-five hour week, which includes three units of study related to their desired job, twenty-five participants undertake a range of work such as furniture repairing, printing, book-binding, landscape gardening and the like. They receive a salary that is £3-4 per week in excess of the basic unemployment rate. The work is sought at commercial rates from the local education authority and other bodies and the programme covers its costs including salaries and the running and maintenance of the factory specially built in the school grounds. The average stay is less than two months — many participants obtain jobs in three or four weeks.

Much the same strategy is being explored in some English schools and youth groups where community skills are learned and undertaken and young people are subsequently helped to set themselves up as 'self-employed' window-cleaners, gardeners, etc., and are taught business and marketing skills to assist them. Grants or loans towards the purchase of tools and equipment may also be made available. In this way, unemployable young people can become employed and services needed by the community remain available. The Tiverton Youth Employment Support Group in the Devon Education Service is a typical example of such a scheme.

The Danish authorities have devised a range of work creation schemes, a typical example of which is in Vejle County, where a project involves collection of waste food with a view to manufacture of animal fodder, cultivation of vegetables in low-energy greenhouses, and fish-farming in the warm exhaust waters from the power stations. Participants work a forty-hour week. There are no prior plans for special educational facilities in the project. If and when requested by participants, however, education can be provided during working hours. Courses have, in fact, been provided in industrial safety and social legislation.

Work creation schemes such as these can only make a small contribution to the availability of jobs; they cannot transform the economic system and are open to many criticisms. One is that they generate 'slave labour'; another is that they focus on low-level skill. Yet a third is that when all schools offer such schemes the over-supply will be so great as to be self-defeating. But in the early stages, at least, work creating schemes seem effective and it would be folly to anticipate or overreact to the criticisms.

Link courses

A less well-known form of school programme is that of the *link course*. In such courses, senior school pupils spend part of their time out of school in the community and vocational colleges and factory schools which are attended by young people already at work. Here the opportunity to work alongside workers and to learn and understand their views is seen to have many advantages, even though it is taking place within a college rather than a work situation. Skinner (1970), Principal of Melton Mowbray College of Further Education, England, writing about such a link course based in his college, comments:

> By a 'Link Course' I mean, not isolated visits to a college, or a purely college organised class, but a fully integrated course between school and college, involving a truly *joint* approach, whereby the staffs of both institutions not only co-operate together in their approach, but are seen by the students consciously to do so, in such a way that each teacher is capitalising on the work of the other within an integrated whole.

Apart from the various specific aims of each course, 'Link Courses' have, in general, four main aims:

1   To bridge a gulf between school and work by giving students a more realistic atmosphere for their studies of the 'real world'. The 'outward-looking' emphasis that is stressed in Newsom can be developed in ways which are not always possible in school workshops.
2   To give students knowledge of employment conditions with particular reference to their environment. Consequently, they should be better able to assess their own employment potential by assimilating various means of self assessment which practice in college workshops makes possible.
3   To make students familiar with the variety of Further Education courses available, to which many will subsequently enrol on either a full-time or part-time basis. They also come to realise the various 'safety valves' that exist in Further Education for those who thought they should change their career aims because they had failed GCE 'O' or 'A' levels or CSE.
4   To introduce students to the diagnostic and problem-solving situations that occur increasingly in the changing commerical and industrial environment.

There are limits to what can be achieved under these aims, but certainly there is evidence that the courses have become an attractive and desirable part of the school curriculum, ranging from IVth form practical and commercial courses, to sharing VIth form 'A' level courses. The youngsters themselves feel this is giving them worthwhile advantages.

This is particularly so for the 16 year old. In the past, he often had to choose between relinquishing the fruits of seniority which he was just about to taste in the VIth form; or he remained to enjoy these yet did not join the course at college that may have been more suited to his needs. By undertaking 'Link Courses', the school-leaver no longer looks upon the college as a 'stranger' which he encounters only when he starts work. He not only already knows it, but through it he should have discovered, *before* he leaves school, the course he wishes to undertake and, if part-time, will ask his employer for release to attend a specific course, instead of discovering this opportunity fortuitously, as was frequently the case.

Work simulation schemes

Yet another form of programme is the work simulation scheme. Such schemes involve the creation of work situation in school. For example, school workshops may be used to set up a production line system in which a basic object — a Christmas card, a coat hook or a toy may be 'mass produced' and in which all aspects of production — product design, market research, trial production, quantity production, quality control, marketing, accounting and much else, may be incorporated. A wide range of experience can be concentrated in well-designed schemes, and many of the determinants of modern vocational identities — the economies of scale, the concept of labour intensity, cost-benefit analyses, and so on, can be incorporated. Such understandings are all too commonly incompletely held by many working adults — even at senior levels.

Douglas (1975) (a subsequent contributor to this volume) investigated a number of these projects and reports:

> The investigation found that school-based factory projects embraced a wide area of activity, ability and experience, involving greater scope than had, at first, been anticipated. For example, two mixed secondary schools in Lincolnshire undertook experimental programmes involving production line projects and demonstrated that the approach was feasible for both boys and girls, while in North Wales a low ability school leavers' class in one school became motivated and industrious for the first time when given the opportunity to produce articles as a viable commercial undertaking.

He identified some of the main objectives of these projects as:

1 To widen the pupil's understanding of the world of industry.
2 To increase the pupil's awareness of the career potential in different parts of industry.
3 To involve pupils in problem selection and solution related to product and organisational design of an industrial nature.

4   To introduce pupils to the planning techniques and methods required for efficient quantity production.

5   To provide the opportunity for increased achievement and social interaction through group or team methods of working.

More ambitious schemes are those of Young Enterprise project which,

> provide young people between fifteen and nineteen with the opportunity of learning about the organisation, management and operation of a business by forming and running their own company in miniature. This helps young people by giving them an understanding of the business world they are about to enter, or have recently entered. It aids them in their choice of career and in the development of their personal qualities of leadership, initiative and self confidence. To enable young people to take part in this project there has to be a sponsor – a firm who will provide experts to advise the pupils on certain aspects of production, management and even lend out some equipment. Usually a 'Young Enterprise' company consists of about twenty boys and girls from local schools and colleges (Ivison, 1979).

In addition to these five categories of progamme there are, of course, many other attempts by schools and colleges to contribute to the development of vocational identity. A typical programme, modest but highly effective, is the A B C Project at Newcastle, Staffordshire, England (A Better Chance). Here potentially unemployable adolescents are offered a course which helps them to assess what they can offer to employers, helps them to 'present themselves' in letter and in interview and above all, enhances their self-concept of ability. A high proportion of all who have taken the course so far have found work – a figure substantially in excess of expectations.

The characteristics of school work experience programmes

All the forms of school programme have three aims in common. The first is to increase the possibility of employment and to ensure a more effective linkage between the role of the student and the role of the worker and to facilitate the transition between school and work so that dissonance and disturbance to the young person, his fellow workers, his employers, his family and his community is reduced.

The second feature of all such projects is that they embody a knowledge content. All identify a body of understandings, skills, values and orientations which, it is believed, are valuable components of vocational identity. All too often, however, this knowledge content is largely determined, if not wholly so, by the adult participants. Yet we are increasingly aware that the understandings of the young people themselves provide a crucial component of their vocational identity and that, unless they are taken into account in devising such programmes, it is likely that the achievement will fall far short of what might have been possible. The incomplete recognition of the highly important understandings of young people is clearly to be seen in the quotation from Willis's work that has already been used. It is also portrayed by Webb in his account of Black School (1962):

> What sort of person would the boy become who accepted the standards the teacher tries to impose? In himself he would be neat, orderly, polite and servile. With the arithmetic and English he absorbed at school, and after further training, he might become a meticulous clerk, sustained by a routine laid down by someone else, and piously accepting his station in life. Or, if he got a trade, we can see him later in life clutching a well-scrubbed lunch tin and resentful at having to pay union dues, because the boss, being a gentleman, knows best. To grow up like this a lad has to be really cut-off from the pull of social class and gang, which luckily few of the boys at Black School are, because both these types are becoming more and more redundant as mechanization increases and job content decreases.

Yet a third issue of school-based schemes is the range of adult participants. Unquestionably, teachers must play an important, if not the central, part in their organisation. Teachers who have previous experience in adult occupations other than teaching are likely to have a particularly valuable contribution to make (though much depends on the perceptions of work held by such teachers). But in addition to teachers, it is important that adults, who are themselves working in industry, participate: it is even more important that these include people who are doing the jobs to which pupils are immediately aspiring. Only in this way is effective and acceptable communication likely to be achieved.

The evaluation of work experience

How may one evaluate the context of school-based work experience? How can we tell if the visit to the factory is no more significant to the lives of the young than a visit to see the lions at the zoo?

We shall leave aside the consequences for administrations and institutions who find work experience schemes invaluable for maintaining high participation rates or even because they can be used to demonstrate that they are 'doing something' to solve a problem. But an evaluation of the consequences for young people is considerably harder to achieve. Overall, young people seem to enjoy work experience schemes; evidence in most available reports suggests that they are seen to be interesting and certainly less boring than other aspects of school. Attendance during work experience programmes often runs at a consistently higher level than participation in 'normal' school. Beyond this the evidence is ambiguous. There is some evidence that work experience is related to a better chance of obtaining jobs in cognate occupations – figures of 60-70 per cent are quoted for some parts of the Swiss *Schnupperlehre* project and some of the Australian schemes. But this placement effect may only be at the expense of those who do not participate in work experience schemes – in fact, a displacement effect! Similar uncertainty occurs where extensive post-school work experience schemes are financed by governments – are the young people on work experience used to do work that is otherwise done by 'normal' workers who are then made redundant; in other words, does work experience *reduce* the number of available jobs? Evidence here can be no more than suggestive.

The vocational identity consequences too are unsure. Whilst work experience may reinforce vocational and workskills in a specific occupation, it may reduce the choice of the individual by inducing 'premature specificity' and run counter to a broader careers education or counselling programme. The increasing dominance of work experience programmes in the lives of young people could well lead to a decline in their acceptance of apparently 'less relevant' aspects of their educational experience. Indeed, the very acceptability of work experience programmes may diminish the overall acceptability of the school. Such realisations account for a good deal of the criticisms of the programmes made by 'regular academic' teachers in the schools, other reasons being the belief of such teachers that work experience schemes divert funds from regular programmes and bring in 'deviant, lefty' teachers with disruptive consequences. Such teachers are likely to be dismayed by a suggestion from Sweden that when three days a week are devoted to work experience and two days to schooling the school achievement remains equal to that of five days' schooling.

This is, of course, not to suggest that the young find all aspects of work experience programmes attractive. Writers such as Ryrie and Weir (1978) show that such programmes can not only accelerate positive work identities but also lead to negative ones and even alienation. Such evaluations reaffirm the need for programmes to be linked with guidance and follow-up schemes: indeed, such a linkage constitutes one of their most significant prospective advantages, though one that is seldom realised fully.

One of the more evident features of all work experience schemes is to emphasise the instrumental rather than the expressive aspects of schooling. Goals such as serving the needs of the economy, helping young people to contribute to society and even 'strengthening law and order' are not uncommonly linked with the practice of work experience. There is some evidence that many students respond to this instrumental approach as in Monk's study of pupils' identities (1981). Yet this instrumentalism stands in sharp contrast to many of the experience goals espoused by teachers and youth and community workers in recent decades as Davies (1981) has demonstrated.

A recurring evaluation of work experience courses arises from the position of their participants in the social system. Gleeson and Mardle (1980) and many other writers notice that there are three 'strands' of young people — those who proceed direct from school to university, college or professional training, those who proceed direct to work or work and training 'on the job' and those who have difficulty in obtaining work at all. Even many schools' work experience schemes are predominantly followed by the 'bottom third', those in the upper band and even in the middle band tend to regard it as a frill — a view often shared by their parents.

This brings us to one of the most important series of criticisms of work experience schemes, that they are no more than a re-styled and updated version of the vocational education programme of the early years of the present century. Though a product of the progressive era of American education, such programmes came to be seen by many as no more than placebos to accompany the process of fitting working-class children into working-class jobs, 'a second class education in the interest of class stratification' (Grubb and Lazerson, 1981). These authors mount a trenchant critique of vocationalism in education in all its forms:

> the goals of vocational education are clear enough — and they are
> distinctly different from the view that education should develop
> every aspect of human potential, including the critical facilities and
> capabilities for self-motivated activity. That vision of education,
> associated particularly with John Dewey, has often been suspected
> of creating dissatisfied, unruly workers who are disrespectful of
> authority, and of encouraging educational 'frills' like art and music.
> In contrast, during those periods when the schools have threatened
> to become 'useless', vocationalism has been ready to reassert that
> all of schooling should be evaluated by its contributors to the
> economic system — and to an economic system that itself is beyond
> criticism.
>
> No amount of training, and especially no amount of skill-specific
> training, can make teenagers eligible for jobs which require some
> higher education; and training programmes cannot reverse the
> growth of secondary labour market jobs which provide some employ-
> ment for teenagers but induce them to be unsatisfied and unstable

workers. To the extent that credentialing is responsible for youth unemployment, then, training programmes cannot resolve the problem.

It is certainly true that school-based programmes can do little to overcome this structural condition of the labour markets for young people as all critics recognise.* Yet to accept such a negative viewpoint as being sufficient would return schools to the passive position many felt obliged to adopt in the early 1970s when, following Jencks (1972), it was widely asserted that 'schools make no difference.' A decade later many researches show the fallacy of this assertion – though the differences made by schooling are far less dramatic and rapid than those anticipated in the 1960s.

The same small but often significant consequences are regularly being identified in the evaluation of work experience programmes. Thus Arai's (1980) report on forty-six experimental high schools identified by the Italian Ministry of Education reported that only nine were aiming at work experience as part of the regular curriculum. He concludes:

> The slightly disappointing results of these ambitious programmes are understandable in view of the meagre material and human resources devoted to the project and of the poor state of preparedness on the part of both schools and teachers. The key to success lies, however, not in improvements of these conditions but in making teachers concerned realise that work experience programmes constitute a central rather than a peripheric part of high school education.

This finding links with those of Farrar (1978) in her studies at the Huron Institute, USA, which show that one of the key features in the success of programmes (however evaluated) lies in the degree of commitment of the participants, not only teachers and students, but also employers.

Farrar, in her summing up, suggests that some of the strongest features of work experience programmes lie in their capacity to stimulate and motivate young people and thereby enhance schooling and its effectiveness. Yet she notes that it is precisely the other 'political' justifications – job experience, improved employment prospects that are usually argued – the very justifications that have been found to be unprovable at best, questionable at worst.

Some of the most important aspects of evaluation are also the most difficult. In two interesting but as yet unpublished studies of the self-image of unemployed youth, Gurney (1980a and b) dispels the simplistic

*An excellent guide to the contemporary structure of the labour market for young people in Europe is Jallade (1981)

view that unemployment is lowering to the self-image. Rather, it is that getting a job is a route to enhanced self-esteem, especially for the girls. She writes: 'Prior to leaving school, girls had significantly lower self-esteem than boys. Those girls who found employment soon after leaving school showed a significant increase in self-evaluation, but no change was found in the level of self-esteem for males or the unemployed of either sex.'

Hebling (1979), in a study of vocational maturity, self-concepts and identity, obtained results that readily link with those of Gurney. Though more specifically focused to higher education, they are worth quoting here:

> Vocational maturity is clearly, although not strongly, correlated with two different factors: work adjustment and a sense of personal identity (self-esteem is included in the latter). It seemed useful to make a distinction between central and peripheral aspects of vocational maturity . . . It may be concluded from our data that vocationally mature students who run the risk of becoming problem cases in higher education, are mostly to be found among those who are not work oriented, have low self confidence and low self-esteem, and do not have a strong sense of identity or have problems with their personal identity.

A number of studies of the development of adolescent identity emphasise that much of the development occurs as a consequence of the establishment of a differentiation from schooling and that work experience, perceived as part of schooling, is no exception. Such studies question the advantage of making work experience too integrated a component of schooling as, for many adolescents, the need to differentiate themselves from the experience would be counter-productive. Baker (1978) commenting on the work of Willis, writes:

> If, as Willis argues, the cultural leanings are strong and are the axis upon which the separation turns, why is this not manifest until the second year of secondary school? The process of affiliating with the lads can be seen as a more conscious commitment to the culture of which they have been and are a part, more conscious because at the same time as the process of differentiation from the school they are becoming seen as, and coming to see themselves, as 'full members' of their outside world. During the period of differentiation, the boy is seen to become 'as of the same world as his father . . . a force to be reckoned with in this world.' Becoming a lad (ie demonstrating affiliation with the alternative ideology) coincides with giving expression to the cultural nexus that defines one's place in and relationship to the wider society. Through resistance to schooling, the 'lads' confirm and express their present and future identity, just as

the conformists confirm their knowledge and identity through support for the institution (and, indirectly, for what they claim to be, and hope to become).

The evaluation of the clients

There is a great deal of informal evaluation by the young people themselves. Very much of it is unfavourable: 'You know all that work experience at school — well it's just a waste of time.' 'A right send up that school visit to the brick works — my mates there were splitting their sides at the things they told the teachers.' Yet there is plenty of evidence that more perceptive appraisals of young people exist that display an acute awareness of the benefits as well as the problems of work experience programmes.

Gleeson and Mardle (1980) report Andy's views which illustrate a considerable capacity to discriminate between projects.

I wouldn't get the same opportunities off a craft course would I? . . . Craft work is too limited . . . there aren't enough opportunities to do really skilled work. Nowadays, most craft jobs are boring . . . repetitive work on machinery . . . where you don't use your brain. I wouldn't do a craft course . . . if you do, you're stuck . . . you haven't got the same chances or choices, have you? You've only got to look around this place . . . . Most of the craft lads aren't interested in their work or college . . . they didn't do so well at school to get on to a technician's course . . . they're stuck . . . they haven't got a future outside craft work. If I couldn't get a job as a technician . . . or something like it . . . I certainly wouldn't take craft work.

It is also evident that a very great deal of the learning of young people consists of the reaffirmations of established beliefs about the nature of work. Delamont (1980), in a study of adolescent girls, notices the way in which girls' expectations of sex differentation in work is powerfully reinforced by their experiences of both work and school. Far from such experiences leading a girl to enter a 'non-feminine' occupation like engineering, they appear more likely to deter her.

Many of the individual teachers also offer sensitive evaluations. Douglas (1975), whose work at Orangefield forms the subject of a subsequent chapter in this volume, writes:

In broad terms, all the projects surveyed showed a remarkable degree of interest and involvement on the part of both pupils and staff, representing a very wide range of ages, abilities, types of school and locations. Perhaps the most conclusive result and the one supported

25

by many of the previous experiments, was the social benefit accruing from the opportunities for team work and individual interaction. This was closely followed by widespread endorsement for the claim that school production lines offered greater opportunities for the less able to participate or contribute at their own level and share in the final sense of achievement, a conclusion supported by pupils' individual comments and by the views of teachers on earlier projects. Appreciation by pupils of the need for efficiency and planning in such enterprises, the producing of greater incentives to complete allotted tasks and the suitability of the method for the quantity production in schools were another three features of the projects which attracted majority acceptance by both pupils and teachers.

Watts (1980) summarises some of the available evaluatory evidence:

Overall, it would seem from the available evidence that the vocational, anticipatory and placing effects are more valued by young people than the social-educational effects emphasised by the policymakers. Of these, the *placing* effects are the most suspect, because any advantage acquired is to a large extent acquired at the expense of other groups in the labour market. In this respect work experience is merely what Hirsch (1977) called a 'positional good': if it were extended to all, its benefits would disappear. In policy terms, therefore, its case has to be argued in terms not of the benefits it bestows on its participants, but of the net social benefit once negative effects on those who suffer are taken into account. A case *could* be argued here for positive discrimination in favour of young people entering the labour market to enable them to compete with those already in it. An argument along these lines was offered by a Project Trident co-ordinator:

'One thing that's been said to me several times by employers is something to the effect that they didn't know schools still turned out youngsters of the quality of the one they just had. They were very pleased to be in the scheme because it had shed light on an otherwise grey area. They knew more about schools, more about young people 15 to 16, and more importantly perhaps at the present time, some of them are persuaded they may perhaps employ 16-year-olds instead of waiting to employ 18-20-year-olds as so many have done in the past few years'.

The *vocational* and *anticipatory* effects, too, are open to some question, because of the dangers of distortion. Ball and Ball (1979, p 39) point out that experience can *limit* choice. To deduce from this, however, that one should restrict experience is clearly fallacious. The remedy, instead, lies with providing adequate preparation and follow-up to ensure that young people are able to see their particular experiences in a broader context.

Such evaluations, loose, imprecise and elusive as they are, are the best guide we have to the achievements of work experience. In this area of education, more than in any other, it is the client's experience and appraisal of these programmes and the opportunity, legitimation and accreditation they offer him which will ultimately determine the size, nature and direction of future provision. In so doing, they will largely determine whether programmes built in and after school will mark the beginning of a new relationship of education and work in modern societies, possibly involving some aspects of a 'youth guarantee' or merely involve an acceptance of the existing structure often offering only palliatives to non-achievers.

Our understandings remain incomplete; Musgrave (1980) makes the central point well in an unpublished paper:

> My thesis is that we must stop seeing the link between school and work as the focal relationship. The link is working not perfectly — nothing ever does in a free society, but at least reasonably well and many existing social forces will force improvement where deficiencies exist. We must begin to redefine work and relate our view of work and of leisure to education so that we can evolve some policy that is appropriate to the probable economic circumstances at the start of the second millennium, a date when those leaving school at the end of this year will still be only thirty-five. But above all we must initiate the discussions that make possible the political decisions that will ensure commitment to a new social reality, which as always we ourselves shall in large part create.

What Musgrave is arguing for is a re-examination of 'life experience' to accompany the changes that we have been examining in work experience. To undertake such a re-examination is an even more difficult task than to examine curriculum, work experience or guidance as separate items. Yet this is precisely the task of the various authors of the papers in this volume which present a range of activities currently being undertaken in schools in Britain, Ireland, Australia and the Soviet Union.

The case studies begin with the Cambridge Comprehensive Schools at Netherhall and Comberton. Hall and Davies describe the effective work experience scheme which is being developed, with one hundred and forty employers participating in offering an extensive and carefully prepared experience of work with appropriate counselling and guidance. The scheme at Comberton, similarly planned, involves a brief experience of work for all undertaken in liaison with a major local employer — Pye Telecommunications Ltd — and a more extended experience for a limited number of pupils with another major employer — Ciba Geigy Ltd. The schemes, like most others, involve a major component of wider 'life experience' as well as specifically occupational experience; at Comberton the experience is that of an expedition in the Peak District.

Parry gives an account of a similarly careful introduction of work experience at Long Road Sixth Form College. This occurs in an impressive variety of locations in an activities week. Her chapter includes a valuable consideration of the achievement of the objectives of the activity:

> From our point of view we see the Scheme as a concentration of experience, as part of our work in guidance towards an informed career decision, as part of the transition toward the world of work and to acquisition of necessary social skills such as fitting into a more adult oriented environment.

The concept of a school-based transition year linking school and work was introduced into the Irish system by ministerial intervention in 1974 and in that year three schools introduced transition projects. Harris writes about one of these, at Newpark School; the only one of the schools to introduce the transition year for all its pupils. In his detailed report the author emphasises, as do other contributors, the particular importance of parental involvement in such schemes and also considers the reasons for the very considerable popularity of such schemes with all categories of students.

Not all school-based work experience has to be based upon industry. Many occupations are to be found within a wider spectrum and Gunn, Moir and White present an account of acting used as a form of work experience. In undertaking their work with 'problem young people' attending the Bristol Education Committee's Bayswater Centre they sensitively explored not only work experience but also important issues of life experience with the group and pioneered new dimensions of drama education that are likely to be of considerable value to many schools. (It should be noted, however, that exceptionally, Manpower Services Commission funds were available for this 'school'-based activity.)

Two studies of simulation projects are offered. One, undertaken at Orangefield School, Belfast is described by Douglas. There were two 'production schemes' in which students experienced, within the school, a wide range of work experiences in market research, project design, manufacture, marketing and accounting. The report demonstrates that, with enthusiasm and commitment, the resources of the school can be deployed in a remarkably effective way to simulate the conditions of manufacturing industry. The second, the account of the Ynysawdre Chemical Company by Naughton, describes a similar but more technically advanced enterprise at sixth-form level undertaken in conjunction with a local cosmetics company. Like Douglas, Naughton writes fully and frankly about the difficulties encountered in the various stages of the project yet presents clear evidence of the considerable achievements that resulted.

An impressive account comes from Marion High School, Australia; a school that has become famous throughout the continent for its forward-looking approach to work experience. Indeed, as Hannaford indicates, it is a school in which work experience has come to dominate the whole curriculum and in which an impressively wide range of experience is made available. All the strategies discussed elsewhere in this book have been explored at Marion, special curricula, simulations, link projects and arrangements whereby young people who would otherwise have 'left' school remain to participate in continuing educational and work experience. A particular feature of the Marion arrangements is the careful tailoring of work experience to match the special needs of the pupils – ethnic, linguistic, intellectual and emotional.

The final chapter by Grant explores the extensive element of work experience that constitutes so dominant a feature of Soviet education. Though often overlaid and distorted by social and ideological justifications, the Soviet work experience arrangements are dynamic and capable of offering considerable insights to all educators in this field.

Together the contributions demonstrate that schools can offer a valid and viable set of work experiences within the curriculum. They argue that these experiences can and should become a dominant part of the curriculum. No longer need work experience be left to chance occurrence in life after school or contrived by other agencies after a period of unemployment. The contributors in this volume show work experience in the school can be effective and, above all, attractive to teachers, students and employers.

References

Arai, P. (1980), 'Modern Society and Work Experience Programmes in Schools', *Secondary Education*, February.

Baker, C. (1978), 'Becoming Adolescent: The Shaping of Identity in the Junior Secondary Years', paper presented at SAANZ Conference, Brisbane, Australia.

Ball, C., and Ball, M. (1979), *Fit for Work?* London, Writers and Readers Publishing Co-operative.

Becker, H. (1963), *Outsiders: Studies in the Sociology of Deviance*, New York, Free Press.

Bourdieu, P. (1972), 'Cultural Reproduction and Social Reproduction', in R. Brown (ed.), *Knowledge, Education and Cultural Change*, London, Tavistock.

Bowles, S., and Gintis, H. (1976), *Schooling in Capitalist America*, London: Routledge & Kegan Paul.
Careers Research and Advisory Centre (1979), *Schools and Industry*.
Coles, P. (1979), *The CERES Project*, Victoria, Australia, The Brunswick Secondary Education Council.
Coles, P. (1980), *Report of the Victoria Employment Committee Working Party on Work Experience*, Victoria, Australia, Victorian Employment Committee.
Davies, B. (1981), 'Beyond the work ethic', *Times Educational Supplement*, Friday, 13 November 1981.
Delamont, S. (1980), *Sex Roles and the School*, London, Methuen.
Department of Industry, 1980, *Industry/Education Liaison*, Industry/Education Unit: Department of Industry.
Douglas, M.H. (1975), 'Industrial Design and Production Projects in Secondary Schools', *Studies in Design Education and Craft*, 8.1.
Farrar, S. (1978), 'The Evaluation of Work Programmes', Huron, The Institute, mimeo.
Gleeson, D., and Mardle, G.D. (1980), *Further Education or Training? A Case Study in the Theory and Practice of Day-Release Education*, London, Routledge & Kegan Paul.
Grubb, W.N., and Lazerson, M. (1981), 'Vocational Solution to Youth Problems: the Persistent Frustrations of the American Experience', *Educational Analysis*, 3, 2, pp. 91-104.
Gurney, R.M. (1980a), 'Aspects of School Leaver Unemployment', University of Melbourne, mimeo.
Gurney, R.M. (1980b), 'Does Unemployment Affect the Self Esteem of School Leavers?', University of Melbourne, mimeo.
Hebling, H. (1979), *Vocational Maturity, Self-Concepts and Identity*, Paris, OECD.
Hirsch, F. (1977), *Social Limits to Growth*, London, Routledge & Kegan Paul.
Hubbert, G.D. (1980), *An Evaluation of the Education Program for Unemployed Youth*, Canberra, Australian Government Publishing Service.
Ivison, V. (1979), 'Young Enterprise – a school industry link', *Trends II*.
Jallade, J.P. (ed.) (1981), *Employment and Unemployment in Europe*, Stoke-on-Trent, Trentham Books.
Jamieson, I., and Lightfoot, M. (1981), 'Learning About Work', *Educational Analysis*, 3.2.
Jencks, C. (1972), *Inequality: A Reassessment of the Effect of Family and Schooling in America*, London, Allen Lane.
Lazerson, M. (1971), *Origins of the Urban School*, Cambridge, Mass., Harvard University Press.
Manpower Services Commission (1981), *A New Training Initiative*, London, Manpower Services Commission.
Monk, M.J. (1981), 'The Classroom Nexus', unpublished PhD thesis, University of London.

Musgrave, P.W. (1980), 'Contemporary Schooling, Competence and Commitment to Work', Monash University, mimeo.

Rees, T.L., and Gregory, D. (1981), 'Youth Employment and Unemployment: A Decade of Decline', *Educational Analysis*, 3.2, pp. 7-24.

Ryrie, A.C., and Weir, A.D. (1978), *Getting a Trade*, London, Hodder & Stoughton (for the Scottish Council for Research in Education).

Skinner, W.G. (1970), 'Link Courses in Colleges of Further Education' Part I, *Survey 4*, Staffordshire, Keele University (for Schools Council), April.

Watts, A.G. (1980), 'Work Experience Programmes – the views of British Youth', Paris, OECD, mimeo.

Watts, A.G. (1981), 'Schools Work and Youth: An Introduction', *Educational Analysis*, 3.2, pp. 1-6.

Webb, J. (1962), 'The Sociology of a School', *British Journal of Sociology*, vol. XIII, no. 3.

Willis, P. (1978), *Learning to Labour*, London, Saxon House.

Work Experience for Young People at School, Stoke-on-Trent, Ceramics Glass and Mineral Products Industry Training Board.

A number of recent publications have offered suggestions for the content of work experience courses and suggestions for the creation of links between school and industry. A selection of these publications includes: *Schools and Industry*, Careers Research and Advisory Centre (1979); *Work Experience for Young People at School*, Ceramics, Glass and Mineral Products Industry Training Board (1980); *A New Training Initiative*, Manpower Services Commission (1981); *Industry/Education Liaison*, Department of Industry (1980).

Chapter 2

Two approaches to work experience at Netherhall and Comberton Schools, Cambridge

Brenda Hall and Roger Davies

Netherhall is a large 11-18 comprehensive school of 1450 pupils situated in the south-eastern suburbs of Cambridge. It has a long-established scheme that offers work experience to many of its fifth- and sixth-form pupils. The scheme grew from arrangements that originated in the separate Netherhall secondary modern schools that existed prior to the 1974 re-organisation of secondary schooling in Cambridgeshire. It was founded by the headmistress of the Girls Secondary Modern some fourteen years ago and at that time about twenty firms had agreed to participate in the scheme. In September 1967 all forty-seven girls who stayed on for a fifth year in those pre-ROSLA days spent half a day per week on work experience, changing jobs at Christmas and again in the summer after exams, thereby accumulating three different vocational experiences by the end of the year. After discussions with the City Education Officer, a specialist post was created for a careers teacher, who was appointed in January 1968 with responsibilities that included the further development of this scheme. By July 1971 over 100 firms were co-operating in the scheme, and in September 1971 there were eighty-four girls taking part.

In 1974 the two secondary modern schools joined with the grammar school for boys and since then the careers teacher has extended the arrangements through the larger, comprehensive Netherhall. The curriculum for the fourth and fifth years is organised so that some pupils have work experience included as a part of their fifth-year course in place of some of their maths, English or social studies lessons. Some other fifth years can choose to drop one of their subject options — this may be a non-examination course that they have studied in the fourth year or it may be an examination course that they retire from after careful consultation with parents and staff. Individual needs are considered in detail before decisions are made. Some pupils and their parents request work experience but find that it cannot be organised within the school week. They may be accommodated during holiday periods or on Saturdays. There has been some consideration of a block of work experience, possibly a complete week for some other fifth-year pupils drawn from a wider ability range. No decisions about such a scheme and its timing within the school year have been reached as yet.

The largest number of individuals involved in the scheme in a school year has been 108. During the Spring Term of 1981 there are 75 fifth years and 13 sixth formers pursuing weekly work experience. A wide variety of occupations is encompassed — working in hospitals, with children, with the elderly, with the mentally ill, with the handicapped; working in shops, offices, gardens, kitchens, laboratories, nurseries, schools, hairdressing salons, garages, workshops, factories, dental surgeries, veterinary surgeries, a sports hall. Many pupils do still change jobs each term, sampling three kinds of work in different environments. Some pupils may stay at the same place if it is felt to be beneficial.

At present some 140 employers take part in the scheme and others are recruited each term by the careers teacher.

Much time is spent explaining the scheme to pupils, parents and employers by phone, by letter, by visits, by discussion and at various meetings. The aims of the scheme have to be made clear. These include:

1   To give pupils some insight into the world of work, the routines of work e.g. regular attendance, punctuality, dress, responsibilities to others.

2   To give pupils the opportunity to experience and adapt to different work situations and become more aware of the variety of work that might be available in relation to their abilities and interests.

3   To clarify their own ideas of employment and view different jobs more realistically.

4   To provide opportunities for pupils to make relationships with adults in a working environment.

5   To increase pupils' confidence by enabling them to experience circumstances other than those prevailing in school.

It is stressed that there can be occasions when participants have to use initiative, work without direct supervision and accept some responsibilities. Some pupils come to see the relevance of their school subjects, of English, maths, the sciences, the crafts; some quote their work experience in oral and written work at school. In some pupils motivation may be fostered together with a greater awareness of the personal qualities that are looked for in different occupations. An appreciation of the need for safety regulations can be sharpened and a feeling of achievement and success is within the reach of all, whatever their academic abilities.

The calendar of the scheme begins in May. Brief introductions are given to two groups of pupils: those fourth years whose fifth-year course includes work experience, and those fourth years who may choose work experience as an alternative to a subject that they have been studying in the fourth year. Letters are then taken home by those pupils, asking their parents whether they wish their son or daughter to take part. If a subject has to be dropped, the matter is discussed with pupils, parents, teachers and year tutors. It is usually the design for living course or a craft subject that is set aside. In a second letter the types of work experience are set out; pupils indicate first, second and third choices and these are endorsed by their parents. This information is sorted and recorded on career profiles. Individuals are interviewed by the careers tutor to discuss their ideas, availability, health problems, general suitability. Discussions also take place with form teachers and year tutors.

By the end of June the placings and timings of each pupil are sorted. Employers have been contacted, and visits made to those who are new to the system. Some pupils are interviewed by employers before placements are confirmed. In early July arrangements are set out in writing. Employers receive pupil details, parents acknowledge the arrangements and give their consent by signature. The careers tutor supplies complete lists of pupils and their placements to the Cambridge Careers Office. Attendance cards are prepared showing times and dates, giving instructions, naming supervisors.

In September all participants are seen individually or in small groups before embarking on the work experience. They are given diary notebooks, advice on how to record their experience, on travelling to work, on what to wear. On their first visit they deliver the attendance cards. Throughout the term the careers tutor supervises the scheme by frequent telephone calls and by making regular visits to the employers' premises. These visits are facilitated by the flexibility of the timetable which allows pupils to go out on three different half-days in the week. This provides more opportunities for direct contact with employers which is also important and helpful in other aspects of careers work in the school. At the end of each term letters of thanks are sent by both the participants and the school. Attendance cards are returned with comments from the employers. Some employers write accompanying letters and offer to provide references for the youngsters. Some offer permanent employment though it has been stressed throughout the scheme that placement is not the purpose of work experience.

The majority of pupils enjoy their work experience and clearly gain from it. They increase in confidence and seem better placed to make decisions about their careers. The employers are very helpful. Some mention that they enjoy the contact with the school and young people, welcoming the opportunity to explain their work. Some comment on how well the pupils develop over a fairly short period of time. There are difficulties. The time needed for organisation, for paperwork, telephoning, supervising, is immense. Travel arrangements can be awkward and costly, though most placements are within reasonable distance of the school and many are able to cycle. Regular attendance can be avoided and absences are sometimes difficult to check, for teachers also assist in checking pupils attendance and progress. There are limitations in some areas of work experience as one half-day a week is not always a sufficient period of time for a pupil to become involved in the work and follow it through, and mornings are sometimes more convenient than afternoons for employers and the type of work experience. The hours of attendance at work experience may be different to school time, especially during the afternoons, and this can present additional problems.

With the increase in unemployment among school leavers and in YOP work experience schemes and with cut-backs in the staffing of schools and local firms it may become more and more difficult to sustain such a range of work experience opportunities. However, Netherhall's scheme is so well-established and so worthwhile that every effort will be made not merely to maintain it but to extend it further, by providing opportunities for a wider ability range and by developing the scheme for more sixth-form students.

Outside the city of Cambridge most of the village colleges have difficulty in attempting to provide work experience on a large scale. Their catchment areas have few employers and only a handful of placements could be made within reasonable cycling distance of the schools. Comberton is an 11-16 village college in a rural setting, six miles southwest of Cambridge. Since 1974, CVC has had a comprehensive intake and has grown in size to become six-form entry with a population of some 910 pupils and 52 teachers.

At Comberton in 1976-7 there was work experience for only four out of 108 fifth years. This work experience was organised by the Cambridge Careers Service. It placed the participants on introductory vocational courses at the College of Further Education in Cambridge and at the Francis Jeeps Farm College in Milton. It meant regular one-day-a-week attendance through the school year, the whole of Friday's schooling being consistently missed. Not surprisingly, those identified as 'best suited' to the arrangement were lads who got little from their formal schooling and were entered for few public examinations.

Within two years the withdrawal of local government funding swept away these opportunities for work experience.

In his multi-role as Director of Studies, Deputy Head (Curriculum),

35

joint time-tabler, examinations officer and careers teacher, the teacher responsible for careers education could not find the time to organise work experience for more than a handful of upper school pupils in the period 1977-9. Fifth years were alerted to the possibility of applying for work experience. Where an individual took the initiative and nego-tiated a place with local employers a scheme would be established, with help, in the later stages, from the Director of Studies and the Cam-bridge Careers Service. Each year some twelve to fifteen youngsters thereby obtained work experience, sometimes for half a day per week extending across two terms, sometimes for a block of one or two weeks at a manageable time of the year. In a few instances schemes were arranged by the school and careers service with no pupil initiative. Meanwhile, the population of fifth years increased from 150 in 1977-8 to 180 in 1978-9 and to 198 in 1979-80. Thus work experience in-volved less than 10 per cent of the school population.

The delegation of certain responsibilities, such as the thankless chores of examinations officer, and the recruiting of a colleague to share careers education seemed to offer the Director of Studies an opportunity to greatly enlarge the college's work experience activities. However, it was decided that the college would not try to parallel the excellent and long-established schemes of Swavesey and Netherhall. There were a number of reasons for this:

(a) Both of the staff involved in Comberton's Careers Education carried too varied and demanding a range of other duties to be able to devote the huge amount of time required to found a 'whole-year-group' scheme like Swavesey's or one to match the scale and variety of Netherhall's operations.

(b) Both of the well-established schemes mentioned above depend sub-stantially on opportunities in Cambridge. There is a saturation point beyond which local industry and commerce, however well-disposed, cannot assist additional schemes on any grand scale.

(c) The developing recession was making some employers cost-conscious to the point of being unable to supply work experience arrangements with the preparation and supervision they required.

(d) Growing unemployment, especially among school-leavers was prompting the Manpower Services Commission's Youth Oppor-tunities Programme response. The very youngsters who had been organised into work experience during their secondary schooling were becoming candidates for work experience after school. It seemed likely that the extension of YOP schemes would minimise the work experience opportunities of those still attending school.

(e) Anything short of a 'whole year-group' arrangement seemed certain to exclude the most academic, those who, it can be argued, may never become professionally involved in them.

Therefore, Comberton developed a double strategy:

Extended work experience for small groups.
Brief work observation for all.

It was felt that pupils of all abilities and attitudes must have some meaningful, eye-opening contact with employment and that college staff and the college curriculum must offer opportunities for all pupils to prepare for and follow up such contact, relating some school-based study to it.

An overall scheme is being established and can be outlined as follows:

Extended work experience

This is of two types:

(a) A continuation of the existing 'sort-it-out-for-yourself' approach, which usually involves some twelve to fifteen fifth years from among those with minimal commitment to academic schooling.
(b) A development of vocational work experience for limited numbers of youngsters with definite subject strengths and particular career ambitions, e.g. some three to six budding chemists placed in the laboratories at Ciba-Geigy Ltd (Plastics Division) Duxford. The strategy is to send Comberton staff on work experience in advance of pupils. Therefore, the head of science, Dr Jim Coppola and head of chemistry, Dennis Coe, spent three days, 7-9 July 1980, at Ciba-Geigy. This enabled them to update their knowledge of the organisation and operation of a chemical company while also determining, in on-the-spot consultation with Ciba staff, possible areas of work experience for Comberton pupils from 1981 onwards. Work experience for Comberton staff at Pye Telecommunications Ltd has been negotiated and, through that, work experience for Comberton pupils with a particular interest in electronics, identified for future use. There are other companies that could be approached in this way but carefully researched and piloted placements will only be available and appropriate to a minority of each year group.

Brief work observation

This is being developed to embrace whole year groups and fit into other preparation for work, preparation for 'life after school' activities that are already well established at Comberton. The village college's 'General Studies' course, the 'Care Course', is provided through extended pastoral time and through the pastoral teams of tutors that are led by heads of year. In the fourth year the second half of the summer term is organised as follows:

1-12 June*   Preparation and revision for 'end-of-year' fourth year formal examinations. Also the carrying out of a profiling exercise in which the pupils self-report, representing their: Leisure interests/activities
Experiences of work in and out of college
Personal qualities

15-24 June   Formal examinations.

24 June -   Follow-up to examinations — return of papers, setting of
3 July   tasks for the summer holiday — report writing by staff. Pupils write up their profiles on report slips that are included in reports that are sent to their parents.

6-8 July   School-to-work conference — all fourth years are taken out of normal timetable and away from teaching staff. For two and a half days they are led by some twenty volunteers from local industry and commerce through small-group exercises and simulations that are meant to alert them to the demands that employment will make upon them. Such conferences have been held at Comberton annually since 1977. Materials are supplied by the careers service and include role-play in management-labour negotiations, job evaluation exercises, job application procedure and interview practice, manufacturing projects.

9 and 10   All fourth years out of school on Work Observation. It
July   is intended that many should be attached to staff at Pye Telecommunications Ltd. The village college is 'twinned' with Pye Telecommunications Ltd (PTL) in a number of joint enterprises with that company. PTL has some 2,500 employees functioning at various levels and representing a very wide range of occupations. To avoid saturating PTL's Site 1 in Cambridge, some of the 195 fourth years have to be placed in other industrial and commercial concerns with which the college has connections. Each fourth year must be carefully placed. Information must be exchanged between the college and the companies. The profiles, the pupils' self-representations, will be forwarded. This will add an immediate purpose and impor-

---

* These dates represent the 1981 programme.

tance to the process of profiling. Descriptions of the job to be observed will be matched against these. The time for this placement procedure is very limited. For the two days each fourth year will observe the role of an individual as closely as confidentiality and safety will allow. Although brief, the experience is intense. The demands it makes upon the companies is great but is restricted to just one week in the year. For the college, the loss of curriculum time takes place when it can best be tolerated. If work observation is to make sense, it should follow the school-to-work conference as closely as possible.

13 July A day mainly devoted to immediate follow-up to the conference and the work observation. Response to the conference has always been assessed by questionnaire. The impact of the work observation will be weighed through report-writing, report-giving and discussion with some personnel invited in from the companies that have played host to the work observers.

14-17 July Fourth years spend four days in the Derbyshire Peak District, staying at Youth Hostels and facing outdoor challenges including hill-walking, cycling, orienteering, pony-trekking, etc. On this expedition the fourth years are accompanied by their tutors, who see their 'charges' operating in circumstances very different from those prevailing at college.

20-22 July Restoration of the fourth year to more ordinary, school-based activities, including those that bring the term and year to a close.

Through this scheme equal provision is made for the whole year group. In one concentrated fortnight they are taken out of the normal time-table and challenged through the school-to-work conference, through work observation and through the Peak District expedition to look ahead to 'life beyond school', awakened to its imminence and to the demands it will make.

All three prongs of Project Trident* are matched, for all upper

* Project Trident was established following a conference of educationalists at Ditchley Park in 1970. It involves the identification of an organiser of links who is usually 'seconded' from local industry and develops any links appropriate to the area. These usually include visits, talks, interview training, sponsorship schemes, work experience for pupils, work experience for teachers. Up to 1979 twenty two projects have been established. Details are available from Mrs E.M. MacArthur at the Careers Centre in Peterborough.

school pupils experience a term of community involvement, time-tabled alongside the fourth and fifth year provision of physical education. Had Project Trident been extended to South Cambridgeshire, the college might not have embarked upon such an ambitious programme. However, it was assured in the autumn term of 1979 that such an extension of Trident could not be funded. With that news this college continued its development of school-to-work conferences and Peak District expeditions and embarked upon the twinning venture with PTL.

It is hoped that the fourth year provision outlined above can be sustained and further developed from year to year. Much depends upon whether local industry and commerce can provide work observation on such a large scale. Moreover, the impact and experience felt at the end of the fourth year have somehow to be sustained and built upon through a fifth year that is the final year at Comberton for all its pupils.

Chapter 3

A first experience of work experience at Long Road Sixth Form College, Cambridge

Helen E. Parry

Long Road Sixth Form College is one of Cambridgeshire Education Committee's comprehensive secondary schools in the City of Cambridge and in the south of the county. It occupies the buildings of, and developed from, the former Cambridgeshire High School for Girls, a girls' grammar school with a strong academic tradition. From 1974 to 1979 the college admitted students of both sexes into the sixth form alongside the high school students who were completing their 11 to 16 education. By 1979 the evolution into a mixed Sixth Form College was complete. The college now consists of some 500 students.

Long Road offers a comprehensive range of Advanced level and Ordinary level courses in addition to a widely ranging series of general studies. Students choose their courses on application, but considerable care is taken at interviews in the spring term, and where necessary in the period after the results, to make sure that the student's course is appropriate to his needs, in the light of his stated career intentions, and to ensure a well-balanced education.

The majority of the college's students are on Advanced level courses with one or two Ordinary levels if needed. Some 90 students follow a one-year course of Ordinary levels, four or five as appropriate to needs or ability. Some of these students continue to the Advanced level course on re-applying through the Collegiate Board. The college does not provide any vocational or sub-O level courses.

Work experience – history

A formal background of work experience was not a tradition of the college; not least because of the lack of time and administrative assistance necessary for its implementation. Many staff believed that most students held Saturday or evening jobs and that many worked during

41

part of their vacations. In addition, there was some feeling that time taken out of an already strained timetable on such activities was hard to justify. These last points suggest some confusion as to the type of work experience appropriate to able students and even to the purpose of such an experience. The part-time jobs held by most of the students bear little relationship to the type or level of work they hope to gain. While the experience is socially and economically satisfactory, it does not, for example, provide any real opportunity for 'job-sampling' and may, in fact, provide an unnecessarily unflattering and distorted view of industry or retailing.

However, on the positive side it should be pointed out that there was a long tradition of community service going back to CHSG days. Through the services of Youth Action (Cambridge) and the careers mistress, many students interested in teaching, nursing and the caring professions had benefited from appropriate placements over a number of years.

In the early days of the college (from 1974) the sole responsibility for careers work was in the hands of one member of staff, a Vice-Principal, who was also head of science and teaching half a timetable. When the Ordinary level courses were first introduced, a second member of staff was given a small time allowance in order to meet their particular needs. This allocation has since expanded a little.

In 1979 the situation changed in that on the retirement of the Vice-Principal a Vice-Principal was appointed with specific responsibility for careers work in the college. He had considerable experience in a variety of educational establishments from work in a University Counselling Service, a grammar school and a comprehensive school and in adult education. He had operated a work experience scheme for several years in his previous school and was keen to start one at Long Road. In addition, the person responsible for Ordinary course students was seeking to widen her experience of careers work and had attended a CRAC Insight into Management Course for teachers and was interested in putting into practice some of the ideas arising from that.

Several of the science staff were particularly interested in fostering links with industry and an Industrial Liaison Officer on the staff had been actively creating these links. It was no coincidence that he had once worked as a chemist with an international company. Science subjects at the college were in process of expansion, with additional staff being appointed and new laboratories built. To mark this latter, a Science Fair, 'Science in Cambridge' was held and an inaugural lecture given by Professor Jack Lewis of Robinson College, Cambridge. The exhibitors subsequently formed the nucleus of our science work experience placement contacts.

So the introduction of work experience to Long Road must be seen in the context of the changing role of the institution, a change in personnel, a slightly changing emphasis in the curriculum and finally, and perhaps most importantly, in the context of what is often referred to as the New Sixth-Former, i.e. the sixth-former who is the product of the comprehensive school system rather than of a selective system, who may not accept automatically that the next step is higher education, or who may aspire to higher education and further training but lack the necessary qualifications. In addition, the sixth-former of the 1980s is acutely aware of the national employment situation.

At the introduction of the scheme, in spring 1980, the employment situation was still fairly buoyant in Cambridge. Employment opportunities lying chiefly in science-based light industry, both electronic and agricultural, and in the tertiary sector, especially in the fields of administration, education, finance and the health service. Clearly, this coloured the range of local placements available to us and it is obvious that there would be considerable regional variation of demand and availability for such schemes. Nevertheless, within obvious limitations of costs of transport and accommodation, it is worth investigating possibilities further afield — this is one way in which our week-long placement has a particular advantage over single-day schemes.

The timing of work experience

A series of circumstances combined to create what became known as 'Activities Week', and to locate it towards the end of the summer term. The major work experience experiment became part of it.

In a sixth-form college the college numbers are reduced by more than a half after GCE examinations in the summer. In addition, after internal examinations there is a general air of winding down as the term loses its momentum and 'whimpers' to an end. A committee of staff decided that a 'bang' would be more appropriate, or to put it another way, that the term should end on an upbeat rather than a downbeat. Rather than the somewhat piecemeal teaching, outings and visits which often mark such a period and the accompanying disruption to continuing classes, it was suggested that a tightly structured week of activities should be organised and offered to the students.

The Activities Week was seen as a period of diverse activities for those students in their first year of Advanced level studies and was planned to extend from Thursday, 10 July to Tuesday, 15 July. This rather 'untidy' arrangement was necessary because of the constraints imposed by certain other fixed events in the college timetable, such as a Higher Education Conference organised by the Cambridgeshire Careers

Service and an induction day for the 1980 intake on the 16 July. Term ended on Friday, 18 July.

Work experience was only one of the choices available to students. Others included some form of community service activity (in practice, the two combined); attendance at an insight into business course organised by CRAC for the sixth forms of the LEA; several low-cost, locally based projects — some subject based, others more broadly based; numerous visits, both half day and whole day and much opportunity for sport. (For the complete list of options, see Appendix A.) The students were encouraged to choose activities taking up the equivalent of four days. The enormous take-up of the options is some indication of the success of the week, in principle at least, and it was apparent from the early stages that staff and students wanted it to succeed. Some 90 students elected to participate in work experience and in a student population of some 225 we considered this most encouraging. It may be of interest to point out at this stage that when the Activities Week was first put to the staff as a whole even those sceptical of the idea conceded the undoubted value of work experience.

Starting points

What did we hope to achieve through the introduction of a work experience scheme? One main objective comes under the heading 'Preparation for working life'. We would not necessarily accept that a college environment leaves students entirely unequipped for the world of work; nevertheless, the fact remains that little is done formally to prepare students. Any preparation is largely incidental. We saw the opportunity for a four-to-five-day activity as giving students a taste of a continuous commitment of time, in many cases to a single task, unlike the fragmentation and externally controlled division of time and tasks as in a timetabled college day. In college, a chemistry-based project for a group of eight students did precisely that. In addition, the week gave many students the opportunity to work as part of a team or a group in contrast to their individually oriented college studies — again the chemistry project illustrates how these advantages can be gained internally but within the administrative structure of the Activities Week. The opportunity to work with adults other than teachers is in itself valuable in developing social skills and in helping many to gain the confidence they lack in an adult-centred environment. We expected our students to make their own travel arrangements and arrange other practical details. We would suggest that these last points are as profitable and as practical a preparation for job and college interviews as any formal lessons.

We approached employers by letter (see Appendix B), highlighting two points especially:

(a) that we were concerning ourselves with first-year Advanced level students, our 'more able students'.

(b) that we were looking at this as an extension of education outside the conventional college framework. In our information to students we particularly stressed our aim 'to encourage you to get into working contact with adults involved in careers you are interested in'. In order to anticipate possible criticism of the timing we added to our letter to employers: 'We are not just devising a way of getting rid of our students for a time!'

It was clear from the large response to the scheme that our offer of work experience was welcomed by students and parents alike and when we approached employers it was clear that they, equally, welcomed the opportunity of dealing with the slightly older and more able student. We were, and are, operating in the atmosphere of general goodwill to such schemes engendered by the efficiently run system operated during the past twelve years by Brenda Hall at Netherhall School for some of her fourth- and fifth-formers, and a more recently introduced week-long placement of students by Swavesey Village College. Our age group, ability range and timing meant that our scheme was not competing with these in any way.

Implementation – preliminaries

On the information sheet setting out the options available in Activities Week, students were asked to complete a form setting out their choices. If work experience was their choice they were asked to specify careers or areas of interest. Consequently, the responsibility for contacting employers was subdivided. The science staff, in particular the head of science, a biologist, and the head of chemistry took responsibility for some twenty science placements, in many cases using the contacts already made as indicated earlier. Youth Action (Cambridge) arranged most of our community service placements such as working with the handicapped in Special Schools. The Voluntary Service Co-ordinator at Addenbrooke's Hospital arranged many of our health service placements. The careers staff scoured the *Yellow Pages*, made inspired guesses, used already existing links such as contacts made at the recent Careers Convention and lists of employers which were provided by the Careers Service.

Some students had made very specific requests, naming specific firms or companies; others were rather more vague, 'something with languages' being a typical poser. Some students went ahead and arranged their own activities through their own, or parental, contacts. These were easily drawn into our administrative process.

It is essential for such a large and more especially for such a concentrated scheme to be shared among several team members but equally important for one person to be responsible overall for co-ordinating the project. It should be pointed out that although we were basing the scheme on that operated by David Elsom (Vice Principal – Careers) when he was at Broxbourne, it was modified to suit our needs. The amount of clerical work involved is very great even for one student, for ninety the task is considerable and requires time, space and an efficient filing system as well as a reserve of stamina on the part of the team. Apart from the initial typing out of the official letters and forms and their duplication, all other administrative work was done by the two Careers staff and the two science staff. That included addressing countless envelopes, heading and signing innumerable letters, filling in the details of placements for insurance forms and so on. The cost in stationery and postage must be measured against the gain to the student. The time may come when we may be under pressure to levy a postage charge to cover administrative costs – not yet, I hope.

In one respect the organisation of the week can be criticised and this was a point raised at a review meeting the following October. By incorporating work experience into Activities Week, staff were drawn into commitments out of college so that relatively little contact could be made with the students or the employers during the week. This was one aspect of the scheme which was not followed through as at first intended. Most of the industrially based science students were visited by the science staff, but the rest of the students received no such visits. In future this is an area we should build on, not least for the opportunity it would give teachers to visit local employers.

The precise timing of the week may be criticised. The closeness to the end of term gives too little time for adequate follow-up. We made clear that the writing of a report by the students was an integral part of the scheme. As with any field-work, the mere collection of data is in itself of limited value, the data must be processed and conclusions drawn and the original hypothesis may then be confirmed and accepted or disproved and therefore rejected and another investigation undertaken. If the exercise is seen primarily as an exercise in 'job-tasting', then the student should be encouraged to clarify his responses to the experience. Most of our students wrote their reports based on the guidelines issued, during a period allocated, namely a tutorial period on the afternoon of Thursday, 17 July. A few were not returned until the following September, and one or two not at all! The intention was to send the reports to the employers. These were, in fact, sent 'warts and all' as they were first written. As a teacher with fairly formal views regarding the use of grammar, correct spelling and presentation, I must say that a small minority of the reports caused me some disquiet, but in the interests of 'verité' they were sent as they were. Perhaps a more leisurely period of follow-up would have enabled us to discuss the experience individually and the reports used as the basis for discussion. While the benefits of the scheme were still apparent in the following September, the event had lost its initial impact and its immediacy.

Inevitably for some employers the July period was inconvenient. The university laboratories were in an unrepresentatively inactive state with only post-graduates working. Local retailers were in the midst of summer sales or stock-taking, with little time to spend on training staff. In this latter case, we amended our schedule and placed the students earlier in the term.

The programme of implementation

(a) The information was given to students and parents after an introductory meeting for students outlining the scheme, in early March. Students were asked to return completed requests forms in a fortnight. (At this stage we were greatly encouraged by an instant response from a parent general practitioner offering to take would-be medical students.)

(b) The process of matching requests to placements as outlined earlier — by building on existing contacts, the address list of employers supplied by CCS, our own resources and parent and college governor contacts.

(c) Approaching potential employers by letter outlining the aims of the scheme, giving the names of students and their declared area of interest and including a reply slip for the employers' use. Of the ninety or so we approached, we had only one refusal. All other employers showed great interest and were only too willing to help. One or two were somewhat dilatory in replying but generally a cautious telephone call brought profuse apologies and offers of help.

Contacting the Personnel Officer, Administration Manager, or, as in the case of the local authority, the Training Officer often proved to be a way of dealing with up to four or five placements and meant that only one person need be contacted in that establishment, reducing the cost to us and lessening the administrative burden. Occasionally, as in the case of the banks, we had to supply references and fill in their own forms.

(d) When the replies from employers had been received, students and parents were informed of the possibility of a placement. The students filled in a brief curriculum vitae for the employers' information and parents signed a consent form in order that we complied with the requirements of the Education (Work Experience) Act 1973 and our LEA's Policy Circular No. 86.

(e) The student details were sent to the employer who was then asked to fill in details of the placement, the type of work involved, the timings, persons to contact, etc. (The details are on the sheet in the Appendices.) This we asked the employers to return to us for the student's own use, and with this in mind at the head of the form we noted a reminder to the students that they were at all times guests of the employer and should behave as such.

This stage was undertaken in June, but it is hoped in future that by contacting employers earlier we may reach this stage earlier so that we are under less pressure as the Week draws nearer. We promised full details of student placements by 1 July, ten days before the start of the scheme. In practice, many students had their details long before this but there were inevitable delays while employers were on holiday, head offices to be consulted, the correct person in the hierarchy identified, or the forms quite simply went astray. In addition, our Careers Service requires our insurance forms to be completed a fortnight before the start of any placement so this is an external deadline we have to meet. From the internal organisation point of view, the two or three weeks leading up to the placement includes a period of examinations for these students, marking and report writing for staff, and in such a period it is often difficult to contact individual students for last minute arrangements.

(f) When the completed placement information sheet was returned to the college a copy was retained for the student's records and the original given to the student. The insurance forms could then be completed.

(g) The students, at a briefing meeting before the Week, were given a guideline on the purpose of the writing of a report and also encouraged to approach the work experience with an inquiring mind and to take full advantage of their opportunity.

(h) A letter of thanks was sent at the completion of the week, actually after the end of term, with an invitation to a review meeting in October.

(i) The reports were finally sent to employers in September with a brief agenda for the October meeting and a request for the return of the reports at that meeting. The response to the review meeting was extremely favourable and we anticipated a meeting of some fifty or so employers.

Reflections and reports

A list of the placements is provided in the Appendices, but it is perhaps worth pointing out the high incidence of medical, para-medical, nursing and laboratory experience made especially convenient by our location adjacent to a major hospital; the specialist industrial placements, especially the agro-chemical, reflecting the specialist nature of local industry; even a farm placement as well as the more usual bank, library or teaching based placements. The distribution might be very different in other regions. Journalism is missing, though we had requests for this; we were hampered by a strike at the *Cambridge Evening News* at the earlier planning stages. (Fortunately they were back in full production by the middle of July and published a very eye-catching feature on the scheme stressing the high level of student involvement.) The language interest was coped with at a travel agency and in the international sales division of an electronics firm.

Earlier I mentioned the role of the student as 'guest'. It should be remembered that the employers have the students on their terms not on ours and that punctuality, politeness, appropriate behaviour and dress can be pointed out by us but for that week the student is answerable to the employer. The reminder that the reports to be sent to employers should be legible, well-written and tactful does not seem out of place. In the event most reports were conscientiously written with a nice touch of individuality. Quite obviously the experience had made most students very aware of their obligation to supply their own follow-up and many in fact sent letters of thanks quite separately from the formal reports. Inevitably, one or two reports caused employers to react slightly unfavourably which raises the point of the place of any degree of censorship or vetting raised earlier.

In referring to student reaction, which, after all, is the main purpose of the exercise and one to which relatively little attention has been paid so far in the narrative, I judge it best to let the students speak for themselves by quoting from their reports – selectively but fairly.

(a) On the attitude of their colleagues at work and the contrast with school:
'I was made very welcome by all the staff in the physiotherapy department. I found the atmosphere at the hospital very pleasant to work in.'
'We were never treated like outsiders' (library).
'The people I worked with were friendly and extremely helpful, never tiring of answering endless questions!' (hospital laboratory work).
'It was nice to be trusted to do useful things and not to have been an onlooker the whole time' (laboratory work).
'The members of the Department were like a community – this I

particularly liked. Unlike in school the work was relaxed' (laboratory work).

'The Director of the unit had ensured that I would see every aspect of the unit.'

'I would like to have been shown round the hospital, no-one offered to take me round, perhaps I should have asked?'

'The whole school went to assembly where I was introduced to everyone, which I had not been prepared for!'

'Teamwork is just as important as individual work, with everyone in each department contributing to one end-product: a happy and enjoyable holiday for the customer.'

(b) On their reaction to the job as a career for them:

'Not everything was to my liking — especially rush-hour travelling on buses after a long day at work.'

'It gave me more of an insight into nursing than any amount of books could have done, and I enjoyed it immensely' (maternity hospital).

'I can see myself in this type of job, as I have had the opportunity to experience the work. It has made me more enthusiastic and determined to get through my exams. and to go to College' (Dietetic department).

'I also know that I can take seeing an animal operated on or treated. I was also taught (sic) not to believe everything I read in the papers because nothing like that occurred in this place.'

'I found many of the other teachers friendly and helpful and found that I could see myself in their position finding enjoyment and satisfaction in their work' (primary school).

(c) On the length of the work experience and the division into two half weeks:

'Four days wasn't long enough . . . they were half way through their experiments when I arrived and not likely to finish them or analyse the data before I left.'

'I think possibly that three days would have been a better idea and not with a week-end in between' (civil service).

'I was quite sorry that I was only there for four days and think that this work experience could be made longer' (hospital laboratories).

'Over the four days I had seen all of the departments' (bank).

'At the end of each day I found that I was mentally exhausted, from both working and taking in what people were saying. I think that the length of the training schedule was just right' (library).

(d) Was it worthwhile?

'I would now hope to use this week's experience in my continuing scientific and geographical studies at school and at University. I also realised that not every problem incurred during the working day can be solved by use of a textbook' (Ministry of Agriculture).

'As a result of the course I am now more aware of what becoming a librarian entails.'

'It is always difficult to get an accurate picture of higher up posts in any firm, because what they do takes time to learn and so cannot be "tried out" by someone like myself. However, I do have a much better idea than I did of what goes on' (Department store management trainee).

'My time spent at the hospital was a great experience, since it was so different from anything else I'd ever taken part in' (Children's ward).

'I learnt a very great deal. Thank you very much!'

Review

At the review meeting of employers and the team in the following October, several points emerged. The great majority of those present accepted that the Week had been a success, but not an unqualified one.

For some employers the experience was fragmented — two half-weeks broken by a week-end lacked continuity. For others this posed little difficulty. Still others suggested the greater value of weekly visits, building up a structured longer term programme, and in direct consequence we have some students doing just that, like the student who is visiting a bank on a formal fifteen-week programme each Thursday afternoon. Some employers preferred an earlier start to the working day than the college time they had presumed we expected. This could be amended.

Some scientists thought the experience too short to give any real impression of the long-term progressive work involved. There also seemed to be some conflict of interest here between persons interested in recruiting and training and students and staff seeking experience and impressions. For some employers the time of year was not ideal. The university assistants appointments officer's comments on the university laboratories has been mentioned earlier and a farmer pointed out that July was a slack time on an arable farm. (His student returned to work with him later at harvest time, so presumably for him the week had a constructive result.)

It became clear that not all work is conducive to the presence of strangers; for example, such a situation may hinder the relationship between a therapist and a patient. This point was forcibly made by a speech therapist. On the other hand, perhaps surprisingly, the general practitioner seemed to have experienced none of these difficulties with his three students. This raises the question of whether or not the

51

employers should interview the students before undertaking the scheme. This is certainly something which could be written into the early approaches to employers.

A benefit of the scheme is taking place even now. A student who worked with a civil engineering firm has taken every opportunity at his university interviews to talk about the work and to show his awareness of the demands of a civil engineering career. Another student, who is applying for a course in audiology, was able to talk at considerable length, and with a confidence new to her, about her experience, which was extremely well organised for her by the LEA specialist in education for hearing-impaired children.

We hope that this is the start of an expanding programme. The timing may be changed, we may free ourselves of the restrictions imposed by Activities Week as a format; a still greater degree of flexibility may be built into it. In a sixth-form college we have more flexibility in the timetable than in an 11 to 16 school, for example. Such schemes may be readily absorbed into a general studies programme and the general attitude among staff, students and parents is conducive to its acceptance. There are flaws to be worked out, but the general pattern of implementation will remain. We are happy for anyone beginning such a scheme to make use of any of the material contained in the Appendices, although obviously changes would be necessary in detail.

From our point of view, we see the scheme as a concentration of experience, as part of our work in guidance towards an informed career decision, as part of the transition towards the world of work and to the acquisition of necessary social skills such as fitting into a more adult orientated environment. Finally, we were very impressed by an employer who declared that the week had been good for him too, a sentiment echoed by others at the review meeting.

Appendix A Information sheet setting out the range of options

ACTIVITIES WEEK

This year we hope to organise a week of diverse activities once the internal exams are over towards the end of the summer term. We hope you will all make the most of the various opportunities and enjoy whatever you opt to do. Please show your parents this hand-out: we may eventually need their approval for the specific activity on which you will be engaged. We set out below a few main points about the scheme.

DATES — Thursday 10th, Friday 11th, Monday 14th and Tuesday 15th July.

OBJECTIVES — To allow you to engage in diverse and different activities on a more continuous basis than is often allowed by the normal timetable.

To encourage you to work at activities in groups, rather than as individuals as is more usual in some academic work.

To encourage you to get into working contact with adults involved in careers you are interested in.

PEOPLE INVOLVED — Everybody staying on into the Seventh Year, those coming back to the Sixth Year, together with any leavers who would like to join in should we be able to accommodate them.

EXPENSES AND PAY — We hope that parents will realise the educational benefits of such a scheme and be prepared to make a contribution to any travel expenses incurred — we will try to keep these to a minimum.
None of the Work Experience placements will involve students in being paid.

CHOICE OF ACTIVITIES — In Section A are the activities which will last four days: you state a preference amongst the activities, numbering your first three choices 1, 2 & 3. IF AN ACTIVITY IN SECTION A IS YOUR FIRST CHOICE, YOU MUST *NOT* THEN MAKE ANY CHOICES IN SECTION B.

In Section B are the activities which last a day or half a day: you are asked to choose any combination of days and half days that add up to a total of eight half days (we will try to ensure that you are able to take part in at least six half days of activities).

SECTION A   PREFERENCE
1 Community Service activity, including Social
   Welfare Work Experience: particular activity to
   be chosen later. Local Transport Cost Only
   (LTCO). Consult DE.
2 Work Experience Placement: please specify type
   of profession/career you would like to see: LTCO.
   Consult DE.
3 Insight into Business Management Careers Course.
   Cost £5. Consult HP.
4 Design and create a biology pond area and garden
   at Long Road. No cost. Consult DT/SL.
5 Write, design and produce a college newspaper
   with photographs. Low cost. CONSULT SD/BC/WL.
6 Ecology Expedition — Cow Green, County Durham
   (camping involved). Cost £40 approximately.
   Consult BR.
7 Learn to sail at Ferry Meadows. Cost £20.
   Consult SR.

8 Industrial Chemistry Project — produce a new compound a day. No cost. Consult PF.
9 A Literary Trip — Bronte Country? Lakeland Poets? Ideas welcome! See JO.
10 Produce a play — or make a film. Ideas welcome! See PI.
11 Home based biology projects. No cost. Consult SC.
12 Lend a hand with the Cambridge Conservation Corps. LTCO. Consult DE.
13 Save a site with Young Rescue. LTCO. Consult LM.
14 Electronics Project, e.g. radio telescope, analogue computer. LTCO. JT.

SECTION B
Maximum cost of any one day should NOT exceed £2.50. Select activities to a total of eight half-days (one day equals two half-days!).

DAYS 1 City Day (DE), visit Stock Exchange, Lloyd's, etc.
2 Sothebys, Art Auctioneers.
3 V. & A., Geoffrye Museum (AM), Fashion & Textiles/H.E.
4 Design Centre & Bethnal Green (AM) Fashion & Textiles.
5 Natural History/Geology Museum (PG)
6 Maritime Museum/Observatory (JAG)
7 British Theatre Centre & Play (PG)
8 British Museum (CS)
9 Play the Development Game (HP)
10 Visit Harpsicord centre and concert (MH)
11 Visit Stratford & play (CW)
12 Castle Acre (SG)
13 Devil's Dyke Walk (LM)
14 Fotheringhay and Mary, Queen of Scots (JO)
15 Visit places of worship of different religions (CS)
16 Biology visit to Wickon Fen (DT)
17 Biology visit to Hayley Wood (DT)
18 Visit the Nature Reserve at Grafham (DT)
19 Lecture and visit to Literary Cambridge (SD)
20 The Economics of the Horse Racing Industry (DE)
21 A day of dressmaking or embroidery — make a fun cushion for your bedroom (AM)
22 Day of brass rubbing (SD)
23 Parentcraft (BH)
24 Bread and yeast cookery (AM)

½ DAYS
(SR) SPORT — indicate particular interests
1 .... 2 ....3 ... 4 .... 5 ....6 ... 7 .... 8 ....
(CW) DRAMA WORKSHOP
1 ...... 2 ..... 3 ...... 4 ...... 5 ...... 6 ......

(MH)   MUSIC
Session of group playing .... Opera film
Prepare for Fauré's Requiem from scratch
Visit to Dunn Nutrition Labs. (AM) ....
Visit to Welding Institute ....
Visit to Sewage Works (SG) ....
University Engineering Department Open Day (DE)
Visit to Computing Laboratory (JAG) ....

— – — – — – — – — – — – — – — – — – — – — – — – —

Your ideas and suggestions.

Appendix B

LONG ROAD SIXTH FORM COLLEGE
CAMBRIDGE

For some time we have been concerned about our most able students being more aware of the world of employment, not least those likely to go into higher education initially. We believe that students in the first year of their 'A' level studies should be well informed about the range of employment opportunities open to them, both after 'A' levels and/ or after a further period of full-time education.

This year we hope to organise work experience for any of our 'A' level students who wish to take part. For a variety of reasons, we have had to arrange the period mid-week to mid-week (July 10th, 11th, 14th and 15th). However, we hope that this will not deter you from helping us by taking a student or two who have expressed interest in activities with which your organisation is concerned. We give below the names and specific interests of the students we would ask you to consider taking.

If you are willing to consider helping we would like to discuss the matter with you either by phone or face to face. Please return the slip below and we will then contact you again.

May we assure you that we take this matter seriously: we are not just dreaming up a way of getting rid of our students for a time!

We look forward to working with you to make the exercise mutually beneficial.

Yours sincerely,

STUDENTS   AREA OF INTEREST

— – — – — – — – — – — – — – — – — – — – — – — – —

Please return to   Long Road Sixth Form College,
                                     Long Road, Cambridge CB2 2 PX.

55

Work experience at Long Road Sixth Form College

In principle we are willing to consider taking part in the work experience scheme and would like to discuss the matter further.

Name   Telephone

Organisation   Ext. no.

Appendix C1

LONG ROAD SIXTH FORM COLLEGE

Dear Parent,

You may know that some months ago we circulated a letter about an Activities Week for students, from July 10th. to July 15th.

Based on personal choice, we have now allocated your son/daughter/ ward .... to a placement at ....

We hope this is acceptable to you, and would ask you to sign the parental consent section at the foot of the attached sheet, which should be returned to us by 9th. June. We shall not be able to send your child out unless the form is returned by that date, and your consent obtained. Final details on the placement will be given by Monday, July 1st.

We believe that this scheme will allow students to extend their general education outside school; we know you will give us your support in this venture, not least by helping with any extra transport costs incurred.

Yours sincerely,

Appendix C2

CONFIDENTIAL

STUDENT INFORMATION

SURNAME	AGE	PLACEMENT
CHRISTIAN NAMES		STAFF RESPONSIBILITY
HOME ADDRESS & TELEPHONE		DAYTIME CONTACT
NUMBER		ADDRESS IF NOT HOME

Telephone number   Telephone number

EDUCATIONAL BACKGROUND

Exams taken:

CSE	GCE O-Level
(1)	(1)
(2)	(2)
(3)	(3)
(4)	(4)
(5)	(5)
(6)	(6)
(7)	(7)
(8)	(8)

Sixth-form courses:

GCE O-Level	GCE A-Level
(1)	(1)
(2)	(2)
(3)	(3)
(4)	(4)
(5)	
(6)	

COLLEGE COMMENTS:

PARENTAL CONSENT

I consent to my daughter/son/ward
going out to
for the ACTIVITIES WEEK.

Parent/Guardian

Appendix D1

LONG ROAD SIXTH FORM COLLEGE

Dear

RE: ACTIVITIES WEEK

We have now collected information sheets on each of the students participating in the ACTIVITIES WEEK, and enclose those relevant to you for your records.

We have asked . . . . to be responsible for the students coming to you; she/he will try to contact you at least once during the Week. Any problems should be referred to this member of staff in the first instance.

So that the students can know the detail of what is happening, we would be grateful if you could fill in one of the enclosed proforma. We will make copies so that there is one for each student. However, where we anticipate that there may be different instructions for different individuals or groups, we have tried to include sufficient proforma so that you can supply us with a separate sheet for each separate group. We would be grateful to have the sheets back by 16th June.

At 4.00 p.m. on Thursday, 16th October, we propose to hold a meeting to review the operation of the Week; we hope that you will be able to come on that day, and will forward further details nearer the time.

In conclusion may we thank you most sincerely for your help; we hope the Week goes well. Please contact us if you have any queries.

Yours sincerely,

Appendix D2

ACTIVITIES WEEK
STUDENT'S PLACEMENT INFORMATION SHEET

STUDENT'S NAME

The aim of this information sheet is to give you an idea of what is expected of you during the Week.

TUTOR GROUP

Regarding your behaviour: please remember that wherever you go you are guests, and should behave as such. You should dress in a way appropriate for your particular placement — details below.

YOUR PLACEMENT
MEMBER OF STAFF RESPONSIBLE
ADDRESS OF PLACEMENT
TELEPHONE   NAME OF PERSON TO CONTACT
PLACE AT WHICH TO REPORT FIRST MORNING
TIME TO REPORT DURING THE WEEK
FINISHING TIME
LUNCH ARRANGEMENTS
TRAVEL ARRANGEMENTS (if applicable)
SPECIFIC CLOTHING REQUIREMENTS
WORK INVOLVED ON YOUR PLACEMENT

Appendix E

CAMBRIDGESHIRE COUNTY COUNCIL
WORK EXPERIENCE

SCHOOL/COLLEGE   RESPONSIBLE TEACHER
NAME OF PUPIL
DATE OF BIRTH   FORM
NAME AND ADDRESS OF EMPLOYER

BUSINESS   TEL. NO.
CONTACT/RESPONSIBLE SUPERVISOR
OCCUPATIONS/WORK TO BE EXPERIENCED

DATES OF PLACEMENT: Start   Finish   If 'day release' tick ☐
NORMAL DAILY HOURS OF WORK EXPERIENCE (i.e. starting and
    finishing times)
                From   To

I certify that, to the best of my knowledge, the arrangements for work
experience outlined above are in accordance with the Authority's
policy circular, and that I have received written consent from the
pupil's parent(s)/guardian.

Signed   Date

The completed form must reach the Area Careers Office at least one
week before the commencement of the work experience placement.

Appendix F

ACTIVITIES WEEK

REPORT WRITING AND OTHER MATTERS

On the afternoon of THURSDAY, July 16th, when you have returned
from your ACTIVITIES WEEK, we shall organise a session for report
writing. The reports which you write on that occasion will be sent to
the place where you spent the week, so they must be (a) LEGIBLE,
(b) WELL WRITTEN, (c) TACTFUL.

We realise that each report will be different, and that not everybody
can write about the same sort of things, but we give below some topics
we would like you to cover in your reports. These topics may also
suggest to you what we think you (and we) can learn from the Week
Out, it is not a holiday, and you will be working hard in all sorts of
new situations.

TOPICS TO COVER IF YOU CAN

1 *What you did* — perhaps this could be a day by day diary, mentioning who you worked with — the departments you saw, the children you helped supervise, or the elderly to whom you read, etc.

2 *Your reaction to "work" in general* — things like travelling, the hours of work, noise, bustle (or lack of it), the attitude of adults, and the ease or otherwise of working with them, people working as a team, etc.

3 *Your reaction to the particular job/jobs you saw* — could you see yourself doing those sorts of jobs in a few years time? If not, why not? If yes, why so? How far did the jobs you saw run over into the private lives of the workers? Could you qualify for the various jobs? How would you qualify if you wanted to? Why did the people whom you met enjoy (or not enjoy) what they were doing?

4 *The organisation of the Week Out* — by the College, by the place to which you went, was FOUR DAYS too long? Did you see what you wanted to? Was it worthwhile? (TACT required here — criticism must be polite and constructive).

FINAL POINTS

Please remember that wherever you go you are *guests*.

Please be punctual, please telephone both College and placement if for any *good* reason you cannot get there on a particular day.

Obey all safety instructions without questions, and be very careful travelling to and from your placement.

Enjoy yourselves and work hard, learn as much as you can, talk as much as you can. We will hear from you on THURSDAY, 17th July.

Helen Parry   David Elsom

Appendix G1

LONG ROAD SIXTH FORM COLLEGE

Dear

ACTIVITIES WEEK

It is our very pleasant task to write to thank you for your help in organising an ACTIVITIES WEEK for our sixth formers. We must apologize for sending you a duplicated letter but we would assure you that our thanks are in no way stereotyped!

We appreciate the time and trouble that was devoted to the students and from our point of view we are sure that it was time well spent.

We had hoped to send you the students' reports on their week with this letter, but we think it would be better for us to read them through first! We shall, however, send them to you later.

In order to return your hospitality we should like to invite you and any others in your organisation primarily responsible for our pupils' week with you to a meeting here at 4.00 p.m. on Thursday October 16th when we could discuss the purpose and organisation of the week. Although the first part of the meeting would be social, we would not anticipate that the whole proceedings should last beyond 5.45 p.m. We hope very much that you will be able to come; please return the enclosed slip so that we may make suitable catering arrangements.

Thank you again for your help and co-operation.

Yours sincerely,

Appendix G2

NAME OF ORGANISATION

ACTIVITIES WEEK REVIEW MEETING
4.00 p.m. Thursday 16th October at LONG ROAD SIXTH FORM COLLEGE

I/We shall be able to attend the meeting.

I/We shall not be able to attend the meeting.

(If you cannot attend the meeting but would like to discuss the ACTIVITIES WEEK with us, please tick here . . . .)

The following people from our organisation would like to attend the meeting:—

NAME   DESIGNATION (e.g. Training Officer)
1
2
3

                    Signed
                    Date

Appendix H

LONG ROAD SIXTH FORM COLLEGE

Dear

We now have pleasure in enclosing the reports which the student(s) who came to you as part of our Activities Week wrote on their return. We are sure that you, too, will be encouraged by the response and sense of enjoyment that comes through: we would ask you to forgive any minor infelicities!

We would be grateful if you could return the reports to us, perhaps at the Review Meeting on 16th October if you are attending: some of the students have asked to have them back and we would like to keep a representative sample, not least to encourage the next 'generation'.

The Review Meeting will be held on 16th October at Long Road, and the agenda for the meeting is as follows:

4.00 p.m.	Tea will be served
4.30 p.m.	Meeting
	a welcome by the Principal. Miss E.F. Haywood
	b the College view of the purpose of the work experience scheme —
	David Elsom Vice Principal (careers)
	c discussion of these purposes, and arrangements made by the College
	d arrangements for similar scheme in 1981
	e discussion of other possible areas of co-operation between the College and local employers

We expect the meeting to be over by 5.45 p.m.

We look forward to seeing you at the meeting if you can spare the time: may we renew our thanks for your help this year; and anticipate your continuing help next year.

Yours sincerely,

Helen Parry   David Elsom
Careers Tutor   Vice Principal (Careers)

Appendix I

WORK EXPERIENCE 10th-15th JULY

Gillian Wing	Cherry Hinton Infants School
Claire Hubbard	Comberton Village College
Lesley Harlow	Park Street, Primary School
Angela Boulton	Audiology Unit, Shire Hall
Heidi Boddington	Stagsholt Nursery School
Anne Davies	Green Hedges School
Melissa Horn	Morley Memorial School
Fiona Gunn	Beach Villas, Travel Agency
Michael Kelk	Cadbury-Schweppes, Histon
Jackie Baker	Speech Therapy Department, Addenbrookes
Sarah Pooles	Speech Therapy Department, Addenbrookes
Clare Bradshaw	Dunn Clinical Nutrition Centre
Carolyn Bell	Dietetics Department — Addenbrookes
Stephen Roberts	Cambridge University Press 10th and 11th July
Carey Scott	Cambridge University Press 14th and 15th July
Julia Barnes	National Westminster Bank, King's Parade
Anne Francis	National Westminster Bank, King's Parade
Tracey Westley	Robert Sayle, 24th-27th June
Deborah Cox	Robert Sayle, 24th-27th June
Simon Willis	Physiotherapy Department, Addenbrookes
Matthew Dale	Ramsey & Muspratt, Photographers
Jonathan Moss	Ramsey & Muspratt, Photographers
Caroline Elson	W. Eaden Lilley, Retail 9th-15th July
Mark Hudson	Midland Bank Trust Company, Hills Road
Deborah Morgan	Central Library
Sharon Leonard	Central Library
Beverly Sweet	Central Library
Sarah Lintott	Physiotherapy Department, Ida Darwin
Karen Pilsworth	Mill Road Maternity Hospital
Kate Thompson	Mill Road Maternity Hospital
Helen Pitt	Occupational Therapy, Trumpington Street
Susan Collins	Occupational Therapy, Trumpington Street
Julie Dixon	Addenbrookes, Hills Road — Nursing
Claire Munns	Addenbrookes, Hills Road — Nursing
Nicola Franklin	Addenbrookes, Hills Road — Nursing
Sarah Stevens	Physiotherapy Department, Chesterton Hospital
Martin Freeman	Ove Arup — New Hospital Site
Michael Langford	Geoffrey Woollard, Farmer
Julia Kingham	Ministry of Agriculture
Graham Snelling	Forestry Visit, Bury St. Edmunds. Day visit only

Jeanette Le Boutillier	Fawcett Junior School
William Rowson	Dr. S. Brook — Surgery/Visits
Annette Jeffries	Dr. S. Brook — Surgery/Visits
Michael Rose	Dr. S. Brook — Surgery/Visits
Adele Sylvester	Museum of Archeology and Anthropology
Tim Archer	Chemistry Department, University of Cambridge
Lee Miller	Shire Hall, Land Agency
David James	Shire Hall, Computing
Nigel Root	Shire Hall, Surveying
Julie Norfolk	Shire Hall, Surveying/archeology
Denise Narimissa	Shire Hall, Law
Margaret Murfitt	Ministry of Agriculture 11th-15th July
David Corteen	Ministry of Agriculture 11th-15th July
Richard Simon	Warren Springs Labs
Nicola Dean	Grove School
Michelle Keeley	Fulbourn Junior School
Gillian Absalom	Rees-Thomas School
Eva Preneta	Addenbrookes's Nursing
Arron Khosla	Pye Telecommunications
Andrew Cleland	Pye Telecommunications
Dipika Bavalia	Rehabilitation Centre — Addenbrookes
Judith Pryor	Red House, Little Shelford
Peter Richardshon	Magistrates Court
Gillian McNally	Ministry of Agriculture: Civil Service Executive
Mark Alderson	Accountants Firm
Bruce Morgan	Scotsdale — Nurseries
Robin Thompson	Grieves, Vet. Surgeon
Mary Frattasa	Dunn Nutritional Centre
Graham Mott	Dunn Nutritional Centre
Michael Papworth	Haematology, Addenbrookes
Yvonne Dalton	Haematology, Addenbrookes
David Corteen	Institute of Animal Physiology, Babraham
Margaret Murfitt	Institute of Animal Physiology, Babraham
Emma Frost	EEG Department, Addenbrookes
Dawn Bailey	EEG Department, Addenbrookes
Michael Marsh	Central Animal Services, University of Cambridge
Catherine Bradburn	Central Animal Services, University of Cambridge
Clare Kendall	Pharmacy Department, Addenbrookes
Diana Bruce	Fisons Agrochemicals, Hauxton
Kevin Levitt	Fisons Agrochemicals, Hauxton
Kevin Taylor	Fisons Agrochemicals, Hauxton
Wendy Flack	Ciba-Geigy Plastics and Additives (Monday and Tuesday only) Duxford
Helen Trewren	Ciba-Geigy Plastics and Additives (Monday

	and Tuesday only) Duxford
Robert Baxter	Metals Research, Melbourn
Stephen Cowles	Metals Research, Melbourn
Helen Trewren	Bassingbourn New School (Thursday and Friday only)

Chapter 4

Transition year programmes in the Republic of Ireland — a case study of Newpark School, Dublin

John Harris

The idea of the Transition Year programme was put forward in April 1974 by the then Irish Minister for Education, Richard Burke.* In a speech delivered at the annual dinner of one of the teachers' unions, the Minister said:[1]

> Because of the growing pressure on students for high grades and competitive success, educational systems are becoming, increasingly, academic treadmills. Increasingly, too, because of these pressures the school is losing contact with life outside and the student has little opportunity 'to stand and stare', to discover the kind of person he is, the kind of society he will be living in and, in due course, contributing to, its shortcomings and its good points. The suggestion was made that perhaps somewhere in the middle of the course we might stop the treadmill and release the students from the educational pressures for one year so that they could devote their time to personal development and community service.

In the same speech the Minister issued an open invitation asking any schools interested in introducing such a year to write to him. The writer responded to this invitation on behalf of Newpark School and indicated interest in exploring the possibilities which such a scheme might offer. A conference of interested parties was convened by the Minister in July of the same year. At this meeting, which the writer attended, Minister Burke outlined in greater detail his thoughts about the year. It was envisaged that the year would be introduced at the conclusion of the junior cycle — i.e. after the first three years in the second-level school, corresponding to the stage where the period of compulsory school attendance terminates.

The year was conceived as being 'transitional' in two senses:

* Later Irish EEC Commissioner.

(a) transitional between school and work for those leaving school;
(b) transitional between junior and senior cycles for those staying at
school.

In each case the year was to be additional to the other years of
the school curriculum and not a substitute for any one of them. The
Minister further suggested that the Transition Year should be looked
upon as the first stage in adult education and as the beginning of
education permanente.

Three schools introduced a Transition Year in September 1974 and
a further five, including the writer's school, Newpark Comprehensive,
one year later.[2] Newpark was, however, the only school to introduce
the Year for all students − i.e. to make it one part of a six-year post-
primary curriculum. All other schools introduced the programme for
one class-group only, in some cases intended as a special course for
'remedial' students. The number of schools in which the programme
has been piloted has been kept severely limited to twenty, although
many other schools have indicated interest in being involved.

The official guidelines for the curriculum for Transition Year state:[3]

1 The Transition Year Project is a one-year interdisciplinary programme for pupils who have completed an approved course for
recognised junior pupils.

2 The project is directed towards the intellectual, social and emotional maturation of the pupil. It is conceived as an introduction
to adult education and to *education permanente*. Transition year
curricula can therefore be designed to meet the needs of:
(a) those for whom the Transition Year will represent the end
of formal, full-time schooling; and
(b) those who intend to follow approved courses for recognised
senior pupils.

3 The content of Transition Year curricula will include elements
of the following.
Social education; moral education; education for living (including
homecrafts and education for parenthood, employment and
leisure); philosophy and applied logic; music and the arts; Irish
Studies; *civilisation* courses for students of continental European
languages; visual education; media education and communications
skills; etc.

It was left to each school to determine the details of its own Transition Year programme and to select the list of elements for inclusion
from among those suggested by the Department of Education. The programme thus devised is then submitted to one of the Department's
inspectors for approval.

In Newpark School the new programme was only introduced after a period of one year spent in planning and preparation. Initially, the idea of introducing the year was debated among the whole staff. Those who registered particular interest in the scheme came to special meetings held in the evenings to work out a more detailed format for the proposed course. At this stage the writer invited a group of five teachers to form a planning team and gave one of them the specific job of team co-ordinator. Over a period of some months this team explored the possible forms that the course might take. The scheme which they subsequently devised has been the format used during the six years that the programme has been in operation. Only minor modifications have been made from year to year in the light of experience gained. This points clearly to the thoroughness with which the planning work was undertaken by the team and underlines just how important advance preparation is if any curricular innovation is to be implemented successfully.

The programme which resulted from these deliberations saw the teaching week divided into two divisions, approximately equal in terms of time allocation. The two dimensions are:

1   Autonomous studies – i.e. courses in English, mathematics, languages and various subject options intended to provide continuity of coursework in academic disciplines throughout the year; and
2   Special studies – an umbrella term to cover a range of special activities which constitute new experiences for pupils and comprise various curricular elements not usually included in school courses.

The 'special studies' dimension is further subdivided into:

(a) a series of lectures, films, discussions and visits within broad overall themes;
(b) a choice of 'working areas' in which pupils follow courses of a practical and participatory nature in 'media education', 'film appreciation', 'consumer education', 'homemaking skills', 'drama' and 'coping skills'.[4] Each pupil chooses three working areas in the course of the year; and
(c) a weekly 'Discussion Class' through which pupils in form groups with their form teacher can discuss their reaction to the various activities of the week, together with any issues of general concern that they wish to raise with the group.

The lecture programme is timetabled for a period of 70 minutes at the start of a Monday morning and for a period of three hours on each Wednesday morning. Over the years a panel of lecturers has been built up, who come to the school and talk about their particular specialism or experience. There are three major areas of emphasis or 'themes', each covering approximately one-third of the school year. The first theme is 'The world of work' and lectures cover a range of aspects of working life from information about trade unions to specific information about career openings, qualification requirements and so forth. The second theme is 'The community', where lecturers discuss a range of community needs and services and expose many of the problems present in society. The final period of the year is spent looking at opportunities available in 'The world of leisure' from sporting to other interests and activities through which people gain fulfilment, enjoyment and satisfaction.

It can be seen from this brief description of the Transition Year course that preparation for work is only part of the range of activities and experiences which are encompassed. None the less, it is one of the most significant of all aspects and this dimension, together with the general concern about future careers, permeates in one way and another many of the aspects of the Year. Pupils are very conscious of the need to look at their potential for the job market, particularly in a time of economic recession. They are keen to explore the practicability of some of their ideas about their future careers. They are able to do this at the same time as they assess their position in relation to the formal educational system. Questions must be faced at this point about whether to stay on at school following Transition Year, whether to aim for specific qualifications or training, or whether it is realistic or desirable to set sights on higher education.

It must be stressed that it is in no way the intention of those running Transition Year that by the end of the course pupils will have made firm decisions about future careers. It is hoped, in some cases, that preconceptions and glib following of family lines or expectations can be challenged and subjected to scrutiny. The desire is that by the end of the course, pupils will be more aware about what is involved in work and about the factors which are important in career decisions.

Work experience

It had not been part of the original plan to include work experience as such as part of the Transition Year course. There had been some ideas about including work simulation programmes, but these had never been formulated with any precision. However, not long after the first Transition Year was in operation, it was felt that the theoretical barrage of information being given about work through the lecture programme required the underpinning of practical experience if it was to assume any coherence from the students' point of view.[5] Thus one of the

69

school Guidance Counsellors who was a member of the Transition Year team undertook to try to arrange job placements. This was a formidable task, given the number of students involved. In the first year there were 112 pupils involved and in 1976, 1977, 1978, 1979 and 1980 the numbers were 135, 132, 122, 134 and 139, respectively.

Despite this difficulty, contact was made with firms who were asked if they could give an opportunity to students to gain work experience with them on one day a week for a period of three weeks.

In subsequent years, however, the job placement scheme was organised on a different basis. Instead of going one day per week for three weeks, it was felt that the experience would be more beneficial if there were better continuity and thus it was decided that pupils would go for one complete week to each job placement, and that in the course of the year they would experience three jobs in all, one in each of the three terms. This approach has been judged more successful and also more satisfactory from an administrative point of view.

The aim is to try to find as varied a list of opportunities for job placement as can be provided. It is important to try to match placements with the stated interests of the students themselves. At the same time, the wish is to give each pupil a *varied* experience. Thus, if they have one job placement working in an office, one would hope that next time they could try something completely different.

From the outset, an excellent response was received from employers who have been most willing to support the scheme. Some openings have been found with the help of parents of school pupils or through personal contacts with friends of staff or pupils. Increasingly in recent years, pupils have been making their own arrangements for placements, subject to the approval of the teacher in charge. This has enabled the school to increase its list of contacts. There is considerable advantage when pupils find their own placements, in that they must go through the process of making application, perhaps going for interview, and generally accepting personal responsibility for all aspects of their work experience. This does not necessarily result in a saving of work to the teacher who runs the scheme, however, because it is still necessary to make contact with the employer and ascertain that all arrangements are satisfactory from both the employer's and student's point of view.

The following is a list of some of the job placements which have been undertaken:

Sales assistant in car supplies shop
Assistant with office procedures and general clerical work in insurance
    company
Assistant in bookshop

Laboratory work, office procedures and advertising for Blood Trans-
fusion Service
Hairdresser's assistant
Messenger for national newspaper
Assistant for accounts in general accountant's office
Assistant in wards in local rehabilitation centre
Assistant in school and clinic for the physically handicapped
Canteen assistant for large industrial concern
Assistant — laboratory research projects — Agricultural Institute
Sales assistant in toy shop
Kitchen assistant in hotel
Teacher's assistant in local primary school
Assistant in wards, office and physiotherapy departments of local
hospital
General assistant in RTE newsroom (Irish Broadcasting Service)
Assistant to veterinary surgeon
Assistant in architect's office
Assistant in travel agency

There is, unfortunately, one glaring omission from the above list.
This is in the general field of trades and trainee apprenticeship. In
this case, although the employers are willing to accept students, the
trade unions will not allow them to do any actual work. It is not considered worthwhile for students to spend a week doing nothing but
watch others work.

Following the return to school, pupils are asked to analyse and
discuss the results of the job placements. They also make a written
report of each job experience. Sometimes, if a placement has proved
unsatisfactory as a learning experience, it will be omitted from the
list for future occasions and new openings are being discovered all
the time. The Guidance teacher in charge of the scheme endeavours to
contact as many of the employers as possible to obtain their reactions
to it in operation and to give a verbal report on the students' performance. No written report is sought, as it is considered that this might
impose too greatly on those whose generosity has been essential to
the operation of the scheme. Occasionally (although this is rare), a
student has proved unsatisfactory, or failed to present himself on
time, or even failed to arrive at all. Where possible, attempts are made
to compensate for such difficulties, perhaps by choosing carefully who
will be sent the next time to the place in question, or by asking offend-
ing students to go in person and apologise for any inconvenience
caused. It is inevitable that there will be some disappointments in a
scheme involving so many people, but the vast majority of placements
work well.

There have been instances where a job placement has led to continuing or temporary employment for pupils. In a small number of instances pupils have so enjoyed the work and have so impressed the employers that they have been asked to stay on or to come back for temporary employment during school holiday periods.

Some pupils have been able to make specific career decisions as a result of their job placements. Some have decided that they have found a niche in which they will be happy to stay. In many cases the experience has resulted in the elimination of a particular occupation from a list of possible careers. Some have gone to what they expected to be a promising job, only to find that the result did not come up to their expectations for it. For others, it has clarified their attitude towards the question as to whether they should leave school after Transition Year or proceed to Leaving Certificate and perhaps to higher education. They have been able to see people at work in offices or factories and, through talking to them, assess the significance of career openings in relation to qualifications needed. Thus, for instance, a pupil who had planned to leave school at age fifteen or sixteen may decide to stay on in the hope of doing well in the Leaving Certificate examination, having seen the level of job he may expect if he were to leave earlier.

One question which is sometimes asked about pupils on job placement is whether or not there are difficulties regarding insurance. Often worries of this nature can threaten the success of a scheme. The Department of Education has informed schools, however, that the school is indemnified by the state for its liability to students while on job placement. It is pointed out, however, that it is also necessary for the employers concerned to inform their insurers that these students are present in the place of employment on the work experience section of their course. The cost of any extension to the employer's insurance cover that may be necessary is met by the Department of Education. The Department's letter, setting out these arrangements, is sent to all employers who are accepting students, and to date this has not resulted in any problems in Newpark's experience.

There is, of course, one difficulty which the job placement scheme creates. It is not possible for all the students in the year to go on job placement at the same time. The control of the scheme on this basis would be very difficult and one would be limiting the use that could be made of some employment situations, where employers are willing to accept different students each week over the period of the placements, which is four weeks of each term. As only one quarter of the year group is away at any one time, this inevitably causes problems for the teachers of subjects where decreased numbers in classes and breaks in continuity pose serious difficulties. It must be admitted that this problem has proved contentious at staff meetings. Nevertheless, following debate, it has been largely accepted that the considerable benefits from the scheme outweigh the difficulties involved and teachers do what they can to adjust their courses accordingly.

There is evidence available which indicates that the job placement scheme is highly regarded by the pupils and stands out among the features of the year which they value most highly. An evaluation study of the impact made on students by the course has been conducted by the present writer. In that study, a questionnaire was given to students in which they were asked, among other questions, to list the aspects of the year which they had enjoyed most. Table 4.1 shows the responses to this question by the student group who followed the course during the academic year 1978-9.

TABLE 4.1 *Aspects of the Transition Year course which students said they had enjoyed (N = 109)*

Item	Frequency of mention
Job placements	87
Working areas	64
Lectures	42
Discussion classes	28
Trips/outings	14
Social opportunities	7
Projects	2
Option subjects	1

Here, the work experience programme tops the list in terms of popularity. In other exercises conducted as part of the evaluation, in which pupils were asked to write essays about how they saw their future lives and about how they envisaged their career pattern, the impact of the work experience programme was also clearly in evidence. The tests were given to the 1978-9 student group at the start of the year and again at the end. A comparison of responses did not produce any evidence to suggest that pupils had changed their minds greatly as to how they saw their future. Few seemed to have changed their minds about their immediate intentions regarding whether or not to stay at school or whether or not to go on to further education. This is not surprising and merely reflects the fact that influences outside the school, particularly family influences, are greater than those within the school when it comes to making decisions of this kind. Yet the test responses did show that pupils had a more mature view of their future, more realistic perceptions of what work would be like. It is the writer's belief that work experience makes a most positive contribution to this process of maturation.

There is a danger in expecting too much of a work experience programme. One may erroneously think that lives can be changed dramatically as a result of the experiences gained. There is a sense in which the influence of any aspect of a school's programme is far less than one might expect or wish it to be. This is not to deny its value. One must set realistic limits to what can be accomplished, however. The limited exposure of one week can give a very superficial view of work, especially as regards knowing what it feels like to stick at something over a period of time. Employers and workmates are generally motivated to see that the scheme is helpful to students and the students may not encounter many of the real problems that starting in a real job would offer. None the less, the collective view of parents, students and teachers is that the experience is worthwhile.

The aims which the Transition Year team listed for the work experience programme are:

1   To give students practical experience in a range of working situations.
2   To have a more informed basis for making a decision about choices of occupations.
3   To encourage an inquiring and critical approach towards work.
4   To be more aware of how others live and work.

The value of a work experience programme is not found within itself. In isolation from the context of a course, it can have little coherence and may not justify the time given to it. The benefit to the student may only occur when the actual placement is over and he/she is analysing the experience in comparison with the reactions of others to theirs. In Newpark's case, the placements give opportunities to test out the validity of arguments advanced through the lecture programme, and give it relevance and application — just as the lectures and discussion sessions give meaning and relevance to the placements.

Thus we should never ask, in isolation, the question: should a work experience programme be introduced? This question should only be asked in the context of a course that is being designed. Then the question becomes: will work experience enrich and improve the quality and level of understanding of this course? Will the students benefit from job placements in terms of self-knowledge and with an understanding of how it fits in to an overall educational experience?

From the experience gained in the job placement scheme in Newpark School, the following conclusions can be drawn about the steps that need to be taken when planning to introduce a work experience programme:

(a)   Establish clearly the context in which the programme is to be implemented — i.e. determine the relationship between the programme and other aspects of the school curriculum.

(b) Agree a list of aims and objectives for the programme, taking care not to try to attempt too much.

(c) Establish clearly who is responsible for the day-to-day operation of the programme; who finds the job placements, monitors their effectiveness and so on. It is important to recognise that this job is a big one, which makes major demands on both time and energy. The Newpark scheme has worked because of the voluntary commitment of the guidance teacher who has done so much hard work. It may need to be specially recognised and rewarded if the work is to be done with sufficient care.

(d) Allow adequate time for planning and for researching suitable work experience opportunities.

(e) Establish clear lines of communication with employers, so that there is no ambiguity regarding the operation of the scheme and also ensure an effective and speedy means of contact if things start to go wrong.

(f) Set up procedures for the evaluation of the programme in operation. Feedback from employers by either verbal or written report is particularly important in this connection.

(g) Keep the list of suitable placements under constant review. Goodwill can be built up with specific firms and if there are ways in which those employers who have been involved can be made to feel part of the school programme, then so much the better.

(h) Ensure that adequate opportunities are provided for follow-up work to a job placement. This can include the writing of a report in which the experience is analysed. There should also be ample chance to compare notes with others who have been both to similar and to different kinds of jobs.

Work experience is worthwhile, provided one is prepared to work at it, plan for it, relate its significance to a broad educational context. In this way it can provide a meaningful and beneficial addition to the school curriculum.

Notes

1 Speech by Richard Burke, T.D., Irish Minister for Education, 17 April 1974.

2 Newpark School is situated in South Co. Dublin. It opened as a comprehensive school in 1972. It has just over 800 pupils, boys and girls.

3 *Rules and Programme for Secondary Schools*, published annually

by the Stationery Office, Dublin.

4 The 'coping skills' course covers various skills needed to survive in the world — e.g. skills of job application, interview, of home finance and budgeting, filling in tax forms, etc.

5 A similar situation has been described by Michael Ryan in his report of a Transition Year Programme in another school. 'The Transition Year 1974/75 at Holy Child Comprehensive, Sallynoggin' in *Compass*, 'Journal of the Irish Association for Curriculum Development', vol. 5, no. 1, 1976, p. 17.

Chapter 5

Bush telegraph — work experience in educational theatre

Margo Gunn, Alastair Moir and Roger White

1 'Isn't it all just playing games?'

In a corner of a darkened dining room in an old people's home, a shroud is pulled to one side to reveal a make-shift stage. On the ground Dracula's coffin is illuminated by a single spotlight. Ten fifteen-year-olds in various assortments of costume hover off stage — just out of sight.

Nothing moves in the arc of light.

Half a minute passes and still nothing moves. The audience of old people stir restlessly.

Behind the curtain, voices can be heard rising with anger. The group of young actors is not happy about something. Those old people nearest the front crane their necks trying to peer round the draped shroud.

'I'm not going on without my teeth.' Jerry, a punk with purple and red dyed hair, shouts in exasperation and moves away from the curtain, accidentally pulling the electric socket from the wall. The single spotlight flicks off, leaving the old people — some of whom are deaf and dumb — in total darkness.

The narrator — from a Theatre in Education group called Bush Telegraph who has welded this group of truanting adolescents into a team of actors in four weeks — steps forward to give his colleague behind the shroud time to placate the ten adolescents.

'As you can see Ladies and Gentlemen, the vampire is *still* at large doing his wicked deeds and he's not yet returned to his grave. By now though, as dawn begins to break over the Transylvanian mountains, he is heading back to his lair — the graveyard at the Castle — and we will soon find his evil body asleep in the wooden coffin in the dark crypt.'

Anxiously, he glances to the side to see if Dracula has calmed down. The spotlight flickers, fades and shines brightly again, as the socket is located in the wall.

The narrator steps back and the body of Dracula is clearly visible in the coffin. White canine teeth from the local joke shop, flecked with tomato sauce, hang over his lower lip.

Two more figures move into the circle of light. Lester, our hero, lifts the wooden stake he is carrying above the coffin, ready to strike down at Dracula.

'Now my love, now!' his girlfriend urges, 'Kill the foul monster with a blow to 'is 'eart.'

Lester lunges the pointed wood into the coffin. A bloodcurdling shriek. More tomato sauce flows from the hole in Dracula's chest. A scream from someone in the audience rises in pitch and breaks into a gasping, dying cough. Dracula sits up, worried that he's brought on a heart attack, 'It's alright luv, I ain't bleeding dead really.' 'It's O.K., she's just swallowed her false teeth again,' the warden reassures him from the back of the darkened hall.

The next day the two producers are drinking coffee and reflecting on the previous night's 'performance'.

'Mishaps apart, that wasn't bad, considering they only had five rehearsals and one session to prepare the props.'

'Yes, I'm really surprised it succeeded with kids of this sort, because "serious" drama at performance standard for fifth form groups is usually just for exam orientated classes — not for the drop-outs. Most teachers would cringe at the thought of trying to do a play with fifth form leavers. They'd be frightened of being laughed from the room with cries of "Bloody pooftah rubbish!" '

'But the difference here was that the kids could actually see a point to the production. At the three primary schools and the old folks' home last night, our group were actually providing entertainment for other people. The boost to their confidence and self-esteem in putting on a play that was obviously enjoyed, is quite noticeable. They'll be talking about it for weeks.'

'Of course, the other thing is that they learnt so much by having to work together in preparing it; not necessarily formal knowledge, but they had to handle the organisation and the planning, they had to work co-operatively, they had to discuss what they were doing. It embraces a very different set of three R's — Responsibility, aRticulation and Reliance, and is much more appropriate preparation for their leaving school than formal lessons. It's a kind of life and social skills training course by itself!'

'Would it work with unemployed kids do you think?'

'If it's useful "life" preparation for fifth form leavers, why not extend it to those young people who have left school and are un-employed? It would be a very novel form of work experience training for a small group.'

After considerable negotiations with the Manpower Services Commission, the scheme was approved as a Project Based Work Experience Scheme for one year with funding for two supervisors and ten young people.

2 Take the shame

In our planning of the ensuing project we had only limited starting points, because our experience of Theatre in Education work was either with a company of professional actors, a group of students studying the subject, a group of school kids, or as directors of youth theatre groups putting on performances, and all we knew for sure about the group we were to work with was that they would not fit easily into any of these neat categories.

We had to have a group who could work effectively together, cope with being 'shown up' and 'taking the shame' in front of audiences of their own age or a few months younger, tolerate the grime and grind common to all touring theatre work, and above all share some sort of spark which would make it possible to use drama techniques at all. We had to select.

The twenty-five or so candidates sent by the careers services ranged from a girl whose real interest lay in joining the Royal Marines to boys who wanted to be farm-hands, and from people who obviously craved the structure and security of office work to kids who had taken care to reject every aspect of the establishment they could possibly identify.

Most of them had no clear idea why they'd come. Tina thought she wanted to be an actress, Andy came for a laugh, Nathan came because he was bored at the local hospital doing plumbing on another work experience scheme and Sharon (who we did not take) had heard it was work with kids and thought it might fulfil a cherished ambition to be a nanny.

Once the scheme was under way most of our referrals came by word of mouth, but at the initial interview stage we had to rely on recommendations from the Careers Office.

By the first day of the scheme we had selected seven from the twenty-five hopefuls. Mel had left an 'A' level drama course and was hell-bent on professional theatre, Helena was waiting to go to university. No one else had any significant academic record. Tina had worked with the mentally handicapped as a member of a Youth Opportunities Programme team, Nathan likewise in hospital maintenance, Philip had worked 'on the buildings', Trace was a single mother whose exams had suffered as a result of her pregnancy, and Chris had abandoned a motor mechanic's apprenticeship. Tina, Chris and Nathan all had hints of punk about them. Jane, Julia and Andy, who were to join us over the next few weeks were all bright, punk and articulate but possessed hardly a CSE between them.

On the first morning, with seven trainees and two supervisors to size up, you could not expect anyone to have much time for cool talks about educational drama and 'what we are here for', so we took them up to the Downs despite protests about 'taking the shame'. Tag and its variations, British Bulldog, Red Rover and relay races (whose stages had to be run variously as crocodiles, snakes and ostriches) were exhausting but avoided the self-consciousness and boredom which might have afflicted us had we sat around having meaningful discussions! It was clear that our greatest challenge would be to channel the group's enormous and diverse energy in some coherent direction. Gradually, we introduced games involving more self-control which demanded increased co-operation and concentration.

The favourite turned out to be wink murder. By drawing straws, or some other secret process, the murderer is chosen. He then tries to 'kill' everyone else in the circle by winking at them without being discovered, or at least before two survivors playing can agree to accuse him/her.

During subsequent warm-ups with a complete group of ten trainees and two supervisors we found this and other trust games to be far more effective than the rougher physical games in focusing the group's attention before performances in schools.

On the fourth day we began to work on some lighthearted improvisations. This was not yet our first production, but just to get them used to the work method and make clear that we had meant it when we said that their ideas would matter. We also hoped they would begin to feel a sense of fun in the work, without which a theatre presentation would never succeed, since we could not ask for the discipline of actors. In asking them to choose situations they knew well and which they would like to present, we should have known that five years of secondary education would have equipped them to expose the earnestness of wet liberals like us! Their first situation showed a group of zombie-like punks who 'happened' to have just joined a Youth Opportunities scheme. Tina, a very hearty supervisor with a 'Bomb the Band' badge, bellowed a stream of instructions about stride-jumping, fresh air, a healthy attitude to work and so on. The response of the punks was lethargic and clearly bewildered. Then Chris, as the other supervisor, gushingly explained that provided everyone understood and trusted each other, we'd be able to work well together and it would be tremendous fun. As the objects of these caricatures, we could not doubt their accuracy, and while we felt rather transparent, it seemed an encouraging sign. They had done it spontaneously, just for a laugh, but in the circumstances it would have been hard to write more telling satire.

During the first week, when we were not playing games, we were painting our hut (a 15' by 20' builder's site office) and clearing out the yard in which it stands. This happened with speed. We went out during the second morning and came back an hour later to find everything — walls, Chris, stools, and so on painted red, blue or yellow. Nathan was complaining about getting his clothes covered in paint and so we offered him a pair of overalls. Much to his disgust these overalls had flared bottoms, which he stuffed into his baseball boots to avoid being 'shown up'. In a few minutes he stomped back into the hut irritated because spots of paint were falling on his boots and came out again wearing plastic bags over the leather. Though determined not to be seen in flared trousers, he was quite happy to wear plastic bags. Despite a highly professional attitude to the work, this sense of what was too 'shown up' would sometimes override other considerations.

The difficulty of retaining the excitement, ideas and situations new to the group was to persist. To keep the freshness of a newly devised sketch when it had to be practised again and again ('We've done that one — You get fed up with it') was harder than finding new ideas. That our group had the talents to produce an effective theatre workshop was never in question. The challenge lay in asking them to provide a product which was consistent and which retained its original fire and energy.

3 'But what are these people, Brian?'

When the audience arrived at our first workshop they found a scaffolding structure festooned with performers, frozen in position as Punks, Skinheads, Mods and Wet Liberals.

The scaffolding represented a commercial music machine and we used the crude device of connecting our audience to it with spring clips on the ends of cables. When everyone was plugged in, we as the bosses, activated the machine. Jane, arms and legs all over the place, screamed non-stop. Helena tearfully intoned 'An-Arch-ee' as she swung from a bar to Jane's left. Below them Nathan and Andy massacred the scaffolding they were sitting on with bits of metal and respectively yelled, 'We are the Mods!' and 'Skinheads rule!' over and over. At the top Chris and Julia — exotic in punky leather and hair pink, black or white (according to the mood of the day) — seemed engaged in some kind of mating ritual. This was the opening sequence of our first workshop *It's Only Rock and Roll*.

Fortunately, for the benefit of everyone's eardrums, the machine broke down. But we, as the bosses, were outraged and threatened Tina, the manager, with the sack, unless she put it into profit quickly. In desperation she turned to the customers (the audience) to help her create a new fashion. In small groups they were asked to work on music and ideas to match the fashion, and the best one would be chosen by popular vote.

This was audience participation *par excellence*, but was also the hardest section of the performance, because it required our group to activate the audience and break through their initial unwillingness to become involved.

What made it even harder for the group was that they were often performing for young people of similar age — which sometimes presented embarrassing or threatening confrontations characterised by Nathan's, 'What's that gert Jitter doing here?' after a time-warped hippy from a truancy centre audience had complained at the absence of Jimi Hendrix from the choice of music. Or by Chris, gulping in terror on arrival at a venue in Bath, 'Oh no. It's Bath Skinheads — we was fighting them Saturday night. We'll all be dead.'

There were often dramas like this before a show and it was understandable that, if our group felt threatened, they would lead the subsequent workshop under sufferance, making it quite clear it was not their idea or responsibility.

There is no doubt they had the most confidence in their own creations. For instance, after they had completely rejected a scene we had written, we threw the responsibility back at them, despite our own doubts about their ability to come up with the goods. 'Go on then, you think up a scene that will show how a management can capitalise on the image of a band.' With only two days before the first performance we were relieved that their scene was actually an improvement on the original, with a confrontation between the 'Teazels' (a 'Mummerset' trio) and the 'Ratbags'. Chris, Andy and Nathan became the 'Gert Teazels', dressed in filthy overalls and with straw hanging from their hats.

> *Nathan:* 'I wonder what they yellow lines were near where we left the combine harvester.'
> *Chris:* 'Aaaargh. Dunno.'
> Enter the Ratbags.
> *Jane:* (Brummy accent) ''Ere, what you doing in our dressing room?'
> *Nathan:* 'We're playin' 'ere.'
> *Jane:* 'No you're not, we are.'
> *Andy:* 'Look, we're playin' 'ere. We gets three gallons of scrump and as many cheese sanniges we can eat, dunnuz lads?'

Chris and Nathan: 'Aaaargh.'
Jane: 'So what. We get £600 a night.'

The Teazels are stunned and after some more questions they call their manager. He has no excuse for the discrepancy in income between the two bands, so they sack him, but not before he delivers his parting shot.

Manager: 'You're a load of has-beens anyway!'

As the truth of this statement dawns on them, they begin to rip their clothes in exasperation. They knock each other's hats off, finding cropped and spiked dyed hair underneath. Their overalls are now in tatters. They have discovered a new image (which happens to be punk) and leave, pogoing in jubilation and feeling they are about to hit the big time.

The point was more graphically illustrated than it had been in our script!

After each performance we tried to develop a discussion with the audience based on the ideas of the workshop. It wasn't always at all easy. 'They're pathetic, these discussions. You're pushing people into saying things just for the sake of it,' we were told once by Andy. In truth, the value of the discussions will always be hard to assess, and whether or not the struggle of getting certain kids in the audience to speak at all is worthwhile will continue to be a bone of contention. But we are convinced that our group achieved things, in discussions, which neither we nor the teachers could have done alone.

In a country school, a girls' comprehensive just outside Bristol, the workshop had gone very well and we were discussing what part 'image' and 'respectability' played in keeping a family together.

Teacher: 'But surely the image doesn't matter. If people love
   each other within a marriage, that makes it easier?'
Andy: 'Makes what easier?'

At which point the audience collapsed in hysteria.

To embarrass teachers in front of their pupils is neither our wish nor our function, but from then on there was a very productive discussion, and unless the school pupils had felt able to relate to our group for what they were in contrast to us and the teachers, then it would have not have taken place. It was just this frisson of irreverence which rang true to the pupils and so broke through the barrier of reserve with which they so often fend off the attentions of actors and teachers alike.

When our work succeeds it is not chiefly on the basis of artistic excellence but through an immediate rapport, in terms of self-image, between our 'actors' and the pupils they are playing to. The latter are still part of the school system while our group are celebrating their recent escape from it. But this irreverence creates its own problems, because their joyous disrespect for the establishment has to be played down to make our presence acceptable to the school, and give its pupils access to our work. It is difficult to maintain a balance between being acceptable to pupils, whilst not antagonising staff.

In their punk gear, unloading the props, our group present an un-compromising affront to the formal system.

'Just *what are* these people, Brian?' demanded a distraught Deputy Head of the drama teacher who had booked our dyed-headed company, as they carried scenery through the main school entrance.

4 'Of course jelly babies have wombs'

Ours is an unusual group engaged in an unusual activity and it would be easy to let its members become specimens to be studied and ana-lysed by individuals and agencies from outside. This is a double-edged problem, since it is often through such interest that funding or the opportunities for new activities arise. But during rehearsals for *A Bed of Roses*, our second workshop, it became clear that the feelings of the group must come first. *A Bed of Roses* dealt with attitudes to-wards women. Members of a Family Planning association and two social workers expressed an interest in coming to see how we were progress-ing. They watched the first section and then gave us an analysis of what they had seen, offering what was to us very constructive criticism. Unfortunately, our group did not quite see it that way. Instead, they were outraged that their work, which had not yet reached perform-ance stage, should be 'torn to pieces' in front of them. After simmering for some time their resentment boiled over into a rehearsal which be-came progressively more anarchic and we could hear Andy screaming from backstage that, 'Of course jelly babies have wombs, and pricks and . . .' The message was clear.

While the comments of the onlookers may have been most helpful to us, we had no right to expose the company and their creative en-deavour as a point of discussion at such a formative phase of their work. As they would be quick to agree, they are not the subjects of a controlled experiment. Their work must be respected as playing a real part in a real community. Isn't that important to all YOP workers?

In Bentry Hospital for the Mentally Subnormal, where we worked regularly, our group was a wow from the first. John, a patient who is 5 feet tall and roughly as broad, was determined to play the giant in *Jack and the Beanstalk and Space* — the panto which our kids helped the patients to stage. On our first visit John went straight up to Chris — bright red hair, earring, one leg orange and the other tartan.

John: 'Why are you wearing those clothes?'
Chris: 'To draw undue attention to myself.'
John: (knowingly) 'Oh.'

John was on a strict diet and he delighted our group by insisting that the giant's treasure trove should consist entirely of Mars Bars, Turkish Delight and Wagon Wheels. Some of us spent a whole session helping him to make this treasure out of cardboard so that he could recover it as part of the plot. He did this by throwing bombs at frequent intervals. One day at a rehearsal he found some wooden skittle balls. Being very heavy and hard, they made excellent bombs. Teetering up to the edge of the stage with a ball held above his head, he would hurl it down the length of the hall sending everyone, including the toughest of our punks, running for cover behind chairs and tables, as he chanted: 'Fee, Fi, Fo . . . what is it?' and finally settling for: 'Fum, Fum, Fum . . . .'

With the exception of Tina, none of the group had met such people before and, although Julia had had to leave half-way through the first session because she was upset by the physical contact demanded by some of the patients, most were soon firm fans of the 'loonies'. As well as gathering props and costumes, they also took minor roles to back up the major characters (played by the patients) when they forgot what happened next. On the day of the performance everyone was a bit nervous as the hall filled up with the other patients from the hospital: 'We know our lot, but whose are these?'

The performance went off without a hitch, except for the fact that the curtains would open and close without warning, as the giant had discovered how to turn the handle.

We have since worked in several hospitals for the mentally subnormal. Everyone is now quite used to these institutions and indeed we rather seem to gravitate towards them. We took Andy to pay his fine (just in time) at Flax Bourton near Bristol and went into what we thought was the magistrate's court. We were wrong. It was Farleigh Hospital for the Mentally Subnormal. But we were welcomed and most helpfully escorted by one of the patients right into the court — next door!

From the above it might appear that the group's work in schools and other agencies was punctuated by lengthy discussions as to how they could further benefit the community. This is not in fact the case! They have never said it, but what we reckon they want from the project is the self-respect derived from doing work that others value and the fun of working in a group where your own ideas can actually be used. These things are not new, but they are hard to come by for school leavers on the dole. A small but important step towards the fulfilment of these needs was met by the pantomime which they devised and staged, almost entirely by themselves, before Christmas.

We were then halfway through our quota of *It's Only Rock and Roll* workshops and, predictably, since we did thirty in all, enthusiasm was beginning to flag. They needed something new on which to concentrate their energies. Despite the Father Christmases and red-nosed reindeer which were out in force decorating the city centre, they did not want to perform anything traditional and decided to devise their own panto. The result was *Princess Precious and The Pirates*. Everyone's choice of character reflected his/her theatrical taste and perhaps self-image within the group. Tina was Princess Precious, the vulnerable, romantic heroine. Andy donned pink tights, a white tutu and a large fan which he reckoned looked like wings, and all this above his habitual army boots. A perfectly good drumstick was sprayed silver, with a star added to complete his image as Fairy Godmother. Pete, who was then a quiet bloke, prone to long, immobile silences, put on our fat man costume and became a cross between Bruce Forsyth and one of the subnormal patients with whom he had recently worked. He played the heroine's thwarted suitor Duke Dastardly. Characteristically, Julia wanted to be a stage hand and a 'pirate that doesn't say much'.

The story was simple. The wicked Cruella terrorises the pirates into kidnapping Princess Precious on the occasion of her wedding to the obese and odious Duke Dastardly. As she is carried off, the princess falls in love with Pirate Tom, the classic principal boy. The fairy godmother faints during the commotion, but is revived and sent by the king to find his daughter. After a life and death struggle with a four foot inflatable shark, she makes it to the ship where the princess is strapped to the mast. Captain Death ('I'm Captain Death and I've got bad breath . . .') takes charge.

> *Capt:* 'Well, Fairy Godmother, before you rescues the princess how about partaking in a little celebration. Come on — strike out the rum lads! Aaaargh!'
> *Fairy:* 'Oh no, thank you. It's much too early for that sort of thing. Disgusting. Oh well, just a tipple!'

She drinks her rum to strains of 'What do we do with a drunken fairy' and promptly falls back into the sea. During this drama Tom swears undying love to the princess and promises to rescue her. When the fairy is fished out of the sea a new romance is born.

> *Capt:* 'Fairy Godmother's an awful long name. What's your first name?'
> *Fairy:* 'Well . . . It's Mavis actually.'
> *Capt:* 'Aaah. Mavis, that's a nice name.'

Fairy: 'What's yours?'
Capt: (very shown up) 'Um . . . Well . . . It's Horatio.'
Fairy: 'Oh!'
Capt: 'Look Mavis I like a woman who can hold her liquor . . . and I think Mavis is a fine name. You come below and Cap'n Death'll look after ee — if you gets me drift.'

Meanwhile Cruella, not satisfied with the progress of the kidnapping, has followed Mavis to the ship. The pirates manage to trap Cruella in a net, during which commotion Tom runs away with the princess. There is then a terrifying pitched battle between the king's troops and the pirates. Of course, Tom overcomes the pirates, rescues the princess from the teeth of Cruella (who turns out to be a vampire) and marries her. Everyone lives happily ever after, with the Fairy Godmother marrying Captain Death and Cruella marrying Duke Dastardly. (Well . . . he's old and rich . . . .) At this point the whole cast threw jelly babies at the audience.

They played the show to CSE drama students, mentally subnormal adults, ESN kids in special schools, and produced one or two touching incidents. In one special school we had to adapt the acting area to the space available so that when Captain Death shouted: 'Where's Tom. Anyone seen him?' The answer came, 'Yes, he's in the cupboard.' Or at Stoke Park Hospital for mentally subnormal adults:

Capt: 'Who's going to write the ransom note lads? I can't write. Can you write Tom?'
Tom: 'No Captain, I can't write.'
Capt: 'Can you write, Jake?'
Jake: 'No.'
Voice from audience: 'It's alright love, I can't write either.'

The definitive performance, however was for a Christmas party in a school for young ladies in Bath where, to our group's blatant disbelief, a head girl flushed with embarrassment gave them a vote of thanks for 'putting so much hard work into making such a wonderful evening'. It was at that school that Cruella when being captured by the pirates could be heard shouting above the fray: 'Grrr . . . Get off. . . . AND MIND MY FUCKING WIG!' But the teacher seemed pleased with the show. 'It's probably the first time a lot of our girls have heard a Bristol accent,' she said, watching some of our boys (their modesty preserved in some cases by a single nappy pin at the crutch of their jeans) mingle with gleaming young women on their way to the school Christmas dinner. We were given tea in the staff room afterwards. Our kids dossed on the tables among piles of exercise books and registers. A staff cocktail party went on next door while Chris, who played Captain Death, pleaded over the phone with the police to let him 'sign his bail form a bit late tonight' as we would not be back in time.

5 'This is me sister and she wants a legal separation.'

Of course, such a scheme isn't just a smooth sequence of rehearsals and performance. No working week anywhere is predictable, but many of the disruptions to our 'timetable' involve matters of great importance to individuals in the group, which may have nothing to do with the work.

When Trace arrived one morning complete with her baby and married sister and *her* baby, with sister demanding a solicitor to effect a legal separation from her husband, we had to decide that Trace's sister was not really our responsibility and put her in touch with a law centre who could handle it! We became quite used to dealing with such 'extra-curricular' activities. When young people live away from home and are earning a 'wage' of £23.50 a week there are bound to be difficulties.

Chris and Andy share a room in a flat in the St Paul's area of Bristol. Every Thursday when they are paid, they put the money into piles, slapping it down onto a table.

'Rent, electric, fire, food: £22.00. Great, that leaves me £1.50 for the week.'

On one occasion, after this ritual had been played out, both Chris and Andy were so angry that they felt they had to write to the Prime Minister.

> Dear Mrs. Thatcher,
> I think £23.50 a week on the present YOP scheme is disgraceful if you take into account the cost of living. In my case I pay £10.00 rent, £5.00 food, £3.00 for a minor offence. This leaves me £5.50 to buy clothes, pay heating and electricity bills, travelling costs and entertainment. You make me puke you scum-filled rat bag, paying £100,000's of pounds on your so called 'defence' while hundreds are *in need*. Yours anarchistically,
> Andy Boulden, Chris Neill

They did not send the letter because they thought she might send the RAF to bomb our hut.

It soon became clear that many of them were so broke that they were not eating anything at all at lunch times. We had never pretended our wages were the same as theirs, but the sight of them making a cup of tea last out while we stuffed our faces (relatively speaking!) wasn't easy to forget. We offered to provide a boiling ring on which they could make stews and anything else that they could afford. The idea was taken up with alacrity. We were asked to look after a kitty to which they all contributed. Rotas were made. Plates and pans were brought in and a weekly menu on headed notepaper, was pinned to the board. The system worked well until one day Nathan came running in to find us.

'You'd better come quick. Tempers are running high.' We went to the hut. Chris was cleaning paint off his trousers, Phil, the 'heavy metal', self-styled technician and chain smoker, was lying on the floor in a state of shock. Apparently the plug on the boiling ring had fused and the stew was being ruined, so Phil had been told to change the plug. He was doing this when his cigarette (that someone had 'spiked' with gunpowder) exploded. Thinking he'd electrocuted himself, he'd jumped in the air and bumped into Jane, who was peeling the spuds. Cutting herself on the knife, she was now dripping blood on to the mashed potatoes!

Much of our job as 'supervisors' involves acting as arbiters between people who find co-operative work, as part of a large group, difficult. It is not so much teaching skills as catalysing a productive fusion of talent.

It is now six months since we started the scheme, and we have had an almost complete change in our clientele. Out of the 'originals', Jane is the only one who is still with us. Nathan left to sell T-shirts on tour with a rock band; Helena left to do sheep-farming before going on to college; Phil went on to a YOP placement doing maintenance with Bristol Old Vic; Mel is assistant stage manager at the Little Theatre in Bristol; Trace went on a secretarial course; Chris and Andy had to be sacked in the end after a series of disruptive incidents that culminated in a practical joke that involved 'flashing' at a garage forecourt on the way to a school in Bath; Tina now works in an old people's home; and Julia left to go on the dole because she gets more money that way.

Having worked with this group, we would like to keep unemployed young people as part of Bush Telegraph's Theatre in Education work, because the currency which passes between our young people and the kids they play to is their common ground and shared experience. This is where our YOPs score more strongly than people trained in communication skills, whose spontaneous infusion of reality is blurred by a time-warped perspective and an academic background. Our ideal would be to have such a work experience scheme running parallel to a small company of professional actors, since we feel that each group would have much to offer the other.

Is such a project merely game-playing — just a matter of filling in a year for young people who would otherwise be unemployed and directionless? Is it just a safety valve for restless energy that might otherwise be directed towards destructiveness? Does it merely postpone the reality of the dole queue and is it just a sop to the troubled liberal conscience of a protestant society? Or does such a work experience project hold any clues at all about the direction in which 'education' should be moving as the twenty-first century looms nearer? Are there any implications for the curriculum in secondary schooling?

As young people begin to realise that working hard at passing exams is no longer an automatic passport to employment, what curriculum models will satisfy their innate restlessness? In *Fit for Work*[2] Colin and Mog Ball discuss the value of work experience in school as a mechanism for preparing young people for the world beyond. They are rightly critical of many such schemes, where the 'work' element is either trivial, menial, or even non-existent, and they argue instead for a system that embraces work as an integral part of the educational process, and makes the concept of Lifelong Education, as presented by Gelpi,[3] a credible possibility. Part of their message is that there are other approaches to 'education' that are very different from the traditional methods of schooling, and that there are 'capability' skills to be developed apart from just numeracy and literacy. As things stand at present educational institutions only focus on a small fraction of the broad area of intellectual ability identified by Guilford.[4]

Phrases like 'education for leisure' and 'work experience', which appear on school timetables, are misnomers when 'leisure' for many is a permanent state of being, not balanced by 'work' on the opposite side of the equation, and where 'work experience' is an irrelevancy in areas of the country where no jobs exist. What it needed is an overview of work, education and leisure time, which transcends traditional thinking in a way that can be demonstrated by projects like Bush Telegraph. It requires educational planners who see the value in what others might dismiss as simply 'playing games'.[5]

References

1 Roger White, *Absent with Cause*, London, Routledge & Kegan Paul, 1980.
2 Colin and Mog Ball, *Fit for Work*, London, Writers and Readers Co-operative, 1979.
3 E. Gelpi, *A Future for Lifelong Education*, University of Manchester Press, 1979.
4 Guilford's Intellect theory.
5 Dave Brockington and Roger White, *In and Out of School*, London, Routledge & Kegan Paul, 1978.
6 UNESCO, *Earning and Learning*, Paris, 1980.

Chapter 6

Design and manufacture projects at Orangefield School, Belfast

Mervyn Douglas

Introduction

Simulated industrial design and production projects in the school have been well established, their success had already ensured that the method would be continued and further developed. With growing confidence and understanding of the advantages and disadvantages of the approach, the teaching staff, including new converts to the project team, were keen to try out new ideas and modify earlier practice in the light of the experience gained.

The following account gives some idea of the various stages and approaches used in projects undertaken in two succeeding years. Both adopted a similar organisational pattern but differed in several important respects which related mainly to the merchandising aspect of the operation. In each case, the pupils were two different groups of mixed ability and the staff team was changed, apart from the co-ordinating teacher. The first project saw the birth of Orangefield Enterprises Ltd, which traded successfully in the design and production of small articles of home furnishing, while in the second, Orangefield Constructions Ltd, emerged to do equally well in Primary School storage equipment and classroom teaching aids. As with the earlier experiments, each project was a self-financing venture, which acquired initial capital through issuing a limited supply of shares to the pupils and teachers involved at the appropriate time. This had the double advantage of preventing a drain on school funds and providing a monetary incentive for the pupil work-force and management. Once again, due to careful market research and salesmanship on the part of the participants, a handsome profit was achieved each time and both school and shareholders benefited accordingly.

Preliminaries

In line with earlier practice, the idea of the simulated designing, manufacturing and merchandising project was introduced during the autumn
term to the combined classes who had been timetabled for the activity.
In each year this involved a total of over sixty boys of varying academic
and practical abilities and, in the first instance, one art/design teacher
with two craft specialists and on the second occasion two members of
staff from each subject. The preliminary stages took the form of several
illustrated talks to the entire group, combined with a sequence of practical sessions to introduce the concept of economic planning and salesmanship. This was based on a modified form of the 'Profit Game'
which had been developed from an idea devised for an earlier Keele
Project training session for teachers. Although this had been tried
experimentally on a previous occasion without success, it now worked
splendidly in its simplified form and achieved the objective of making
the pupils more conscious of the need for economy, market demands
and cost effectiveness.

As this was a significant initial preparation for the later stages, a
brief account of the method would seem to be appropriate here. Each
class was introduced to this as part of a specialised competition in the
form of a designing and making exercise for older pupils. What was
required was enough knowledge of materials and techniques to assess
the method of making an article and its potential for mass production
compared with another. The pupils were told that the evaluation of
the design would follow a commercial pattern and were provided with
a list of some thirty assorted materials ranging from tissue paper and
cardboard to plywood and tinplate or processes involving staff assistance, all of which were costed in terms of units. Technical judgments
had to be sound, the suitability for quantity production established,
the appearance attractive to potential customers and the article priced
in terms of units related to the materials used. At the end of the prescribed period (scheduled to take place by half-term) the items would
be assembled together in a 'market place' and the product which sold
in the greatest numbers to the consumers (other pupils and staff) and
which showed the greatest profit, would be adjudged the winner. The
profit margin for each item was to be determined by calculating the
difference between the selling price (which included 25 per cent for
labour costs) and a standard grant of 200 units given initially to each
individual or team of two.

The following is an extract from the typewritten brief given to every
pupil taking part in the second project and differs only from the
previous year's one in that the previous year's problem referred to a
small storage container as distinct from a toy, game or puzzle:

Problem You are asked to design and make a three dimensional toy, game or puzzle suitable for you or a younger person, which might be considered the most desirable thing for you *and* the largest number of other people. It must fit within the capacity of 1000 cu. cms. Ideas should be presented as a prototype, preferably full size, and in the real materials if possible. If not, a *scaled down model* in simulated materials may be submitted.

Method
1   Each member of the class (group) or *team of two* is to produce ONE finished design.
2   Each member or team has 200 units to purchase materials from the price list provided.
3   There will be a time limit for designing and making the objects, which will be arranged and indicated to you by the staff in charge.

Evaluation
1   The finished design is a *prototype* for sale by order to teachers and other pupils.
2   Each product is to be priced – the selling price *must equal* the exact purchase price of the materials used in units together with a 25% surcharge to cover labour costs.
3   Accounts must be kept for checking. If a model in simulated material is made, the price *must* be based on the costs of the real materials.
4   The profit is the number of units remaining from the original 200, multiplied by the number of individual products 'sold'.
Free Offer. Use of hand tools. Advice on production methods by staff.

This method was adopted each time and, not only worked most satisfactorily, but provided the initial incentive and training to allow the project groups to embark on the investigatory stages of the actual undertaking during the second half of the autumn term.

Investigations

In the resurgence of interest and enthusiasm following the successful conclusion of the Profit Game, the boys participating in each year's project were keen to reach the stage of identifying a market need and meeting a potential demand with a suitable product. This involved joint discussions with all the groups contributing and included specialist advice and assistance from the economics teacher. Eventually, the 'market' areas were agreed and a broad range of possible items suggested which, in turn, formed the basis for a market research questionnaire.

It was at this point that the market areas chosen were to differ over the two years being described and although, in the main, the procedures followed were the same, rather different experiences resulted for the pupils. In the first project, the market research was conducted with the co-operation of school parents and concerned a range of possible storage containers for use in the home. Initially, the list from which people were asked to indicate their preferences, covered the following items: tea bag dispenser, letter rack, magazine rack, tape-cassette holder, ceramic ash tray, money box, fishing tackle box and kitchen roll holder. Other information which was requested covered such things as choice of material, colour or finish and acceptable price ranges. The compiling of this information, obtained by distributing the questionnaires throughout the school third form, took place before Christmas and resulted in narrowing the field down to four possible products, magazine rack, kitchen roll holder, letter rack and tape cassette holder. This now allowed the staff to produce design briefs for the pupils to commence work on their solutions in drawn and model form, prior to selection on the same basis as the Profit Game, a preferential voting system involving staff, parents, selected senior pupils and other adults. In the final analysis, two of the suggested designs proved to be the most popular choice, namely a kitchen roll holder in wood and a plastic-coated metal magazine rack.

The subsequent Factory Project was an even more ambitious scheme, which emerged from a decision by the pupils to carry out their market research in the contributory primary schools of the area. On this occasion the possible products for consideration by the primary teachers were mainly individual or class teaching aids, manipulation or sense training toys, classroom storage equipment or group play aids. Additional information about materials, price and colour or finish was also sought, together with an agreement to participate or otherwise in the final selection of the most appropriate designs at exhibitions of the pupils' solutions. Owing to the need for groups of pupils to visit each of the eight schools involved, a somewhat longer time was spent on the market research programme, so that design briefs could not be compiled until nearly the end of January. Nevertheless, with the necessary information analysed and the pupils' briefs distributed, the initial designing and planning stage got under way in due course, with the boys either working individually or in pairs in each of the four activity areas — two art studios and two workshops. To clarify the objectives and various procedures involved the following facsimile of a pupil's design brief is appended. (See Appendix A)

By the end of the term the majority of models, drawings and advertising literature or publicity aids were complete and plans were made to take a touring exhibition of the thirty-four products round the primary schools to enlist the aid of their teachers to establish the most saleable items, using the preferential voting system previously adopted. In due course this system was carried out quite satisfactorily with the support and co-operation of respective primary school staffs. The arrangement which seemed to suit best was for the exhibition to be left for a few days at each school, during which time the teachers had time to scrutinise the wide variety of designs on show and make a selection, using the voting slips provided. Eventually, three widely differing products emerged as the most favoured designs, an adjustable book rack, a shoe lacer (which was a child's training aid) and a set of number recognition cards for classroom use. The first two items were the result of team efforts with two pupils in each case co-operating while in the third instance, one boy produced the idea.

Preparations

At this point in each of the two Factory Projects the work-force was divided into three teams, all with clearly defined objectives to achieve by certain pre-determined dates. The most vital and obviously most urgently required job was in each case the production of a full-size prototype. This was clearly the responsibility of the design team, headed by those pupils who had initially designed the articles, which it was intended to manufacture. A second group took on the responsibility for sales and advertising and commenced with the designing and printing of the share certificates on the school press. Meanwhile, the third team, whose major role was to identify and organise the production processes, started to identify the manufacturing stages, devise jigs and work out flow charts.

In both cases it was about now that capital for the purchase of raw materials had to become available and consequently one hundred shares were issued and sold to the participating pupils and staff. Thus Orangefield Enterprises Ltd, was launched in the first year and Orangefield Constructions Ltd, in the second. On each occasion the full issue of shares was quickly sold and sufficient cash became available to purchase all the materials required, when the sales teams returned their orders. The quantitative analysis required to establish the amount of material needed to produce the articles was the responsibility of boys in the production section and was aided by staff in the economics, maths and craft departments. In both projects, profit margins had already been fixed at the earlier stage but bulk ordering and trade discounts, coupled with substantial orders, especially for the second, were able to enhance the eventual return. With the latter undertaking, staff in seven of the eight neighbouring primary schools had eventually placed firm orders so that targets for the Factory Week, scheduled for early June, were known well in advance. Provided these could be met, shareholders were clearly assured of an attractive return on their investment, especially as it was known that the company would be liquidated at the end of that month and all assets realised.

To give some idea of the quantities involved, it may be interesting to quote some of the statistics relating to the latter project, so that the scope of the operation can be illustrated. In that case, 88 orders were placed for the shoe lacer, retailing at 30p, 22 for the number recognition set at £1.00 and 68 for the adjustable book rack priced at 75p. Production targets therefore were fixed at ninety, twenty-four and seventy respectively, giving an impressive total of 184 articles to be manufactured. Rather smaller numbers were involved in the former project where only two articles, the magazine rack and the kitchen roll holder, involved somewhat more construction stages and consequently limited the overall production figures.

In the month immediately preceding the Factory Week there was increasing activity in each of the three main working teams or 'company divisions', for the respective projects. Thus the design teams were responsible for full-size working drawings and in one instance, (the number recognition set) a package design in the form of a box with suitably decorated label. The sales and advertising groups on each occasion were looking after publicity material and, in particular, sales or instruction leaflets, while the production teams were devising and constructing suitable construction jigs. Again, as the Factory Week approached, enthusiasm mounted and all the pupils became more and more involved with the arrangements and interested in taking part.

Production

As with the previous schemes, the pupils concerned with these particular projects were released from their normal school timetable and worked at previously specified bases or stations relating to the production line, under the supervision of the project teachers, during the specified week. In the first enterprise, this involved three teachers and two workshop areas, while in the second, three of the four project staff, two workshops and a design studio area were utilised. In line with the practice established in earlier years, the boys were permitted to come in casual dress, have canteen facilities in one of the rooms and were required to check in and out for the working sessions each day. Interestingly enough, in the second project, some eight boys in one of the two classes had failed to participate satisfactorily during the designing stage and, on the advice of the teacher concerned, had not been allowed to continue. This sub-group had subsequently been taken as a separate section for a programme of alternative activities. In effect, this reduced the potential labour force from seventy to sixty-two during the production week and this small group, who had, in effect, been 'sacked' for inefficiency, was attached to other classes during that period.

Again, production targets were generally met within the time allocated, although in the second undertaking, some technical problems relating to thermo-plastic techniques delayed the completion until the following week. Apart from that and a few minor organisational hitches, both Factory Weeks proved successful and were supported enthusiastically by the pupil labour force and staff 'management' on each occasion. The timing of the production period to coincide with the commencement of the public examination timetable also meant that fewer teachers were required to cover the classes of those staff directly involved with the projects and consequently reduced possible disruption to a minimum.

Conclusions

Many of the findings which emerged from the earlier experiments in this field were to materialise again during the two Factory Projects just described. The increased social development of the groups and individuals was again a significant feature and the idea of a commercial co-operative undertaking, involving the appreciation of share capital, clearly provided a useful incentive and underlined the need for careful market research and business methods. Quality control was an important element on each occasion and was satisfactorily supervised by the staff concerned. Apart from the item in the second project which ran into some technical problems of manufacture, the standard of finish and workmanship was very high and all the customers were well pleased with their eventual purchases. In this one case, as the staff felt the product was not as well finished as the prototype, the selling price was reduced. The idea of raising capital through the issue of shares and the prospect of redeeming these later with a substantial dividend, appealed greatly to the boys and gave a sense of direction to their efforts. In the latter scheme, the one hundred shares were released at 20p each and this, together with a small additional loan from the school (nominally the 'bank'), met the initial outlay on materials. With a gross income of almost £100, shares were eventually worth three times their face value and were exchanged back at that rate, once deliveries had been made and the money recouped by the sales force. There was little doubt that this gave great satisfaction to all the pupils who took part but, better still, the educational value of modelling their activity on the industrial procedures of the 'real world' was appreciated by all.

Appendix A

ORANGEFIELD BOYS' SCHOOL, BELFAST
FACTORY PROJECT DESIGN BRIEFS

Pupil's Name . . . . Class . . . . Age . . . .

General Objectives. The results of the market research recently conducted by means of teacher questionnaires in our neighbouring primary schools showed that the category of items considered to be most saleable was *Classroom Storage Equipment.* Two others were also strongly supported, namely, *Pupils' counting Aids and Class Teaching Aids.* Examination of the returns showed that the most popular items requested were as follows:— In the first category, Book Racks or Book Storage units, Holders for Scissors, Brushes etc. Containers or boxes for large paper or other items and Tidy boxes. In the second group Abaci and 24 Hr. Clock Faces while in the third, demonstration Clock Faces (large) and Folding Screens were mentioned.

Problem. You are required either individually or as a group to produce a design for ONE of these, in sketch and model form, to be presented for selection early next term. Your ideas should be shown as a full size or scale model together with an accurate orthographic drawing and accompanied by any necessary advertising material and the estimated ACTUAL cost of the article.

Selection will be on the same basis as before, a preferential voting system involving the staff of the participating primary schools at special exhibitions of your solutions. The successful designer(s) will be required to subsequently produce a full size PROTOTYPE in the actual material chosen together with full size working drawings. Eventually the chosen solution will be produced in the quantity required following a sales campaign and employing production line techniques during a Factory Week later in the summer term.

Materials and Cost. Although the preliminary models may be constructed in easily worked materials such as Balsa Wood and Cardboard, more durable stuff must be employed for the finished products. A variety of materials may be employed either singly or in combination with each other. Wood and Plastic were the two generally preferred by the primary teachers as being the most appropriate for use with younger children. Care should be taken in the choice of such materials to ensure that no complicated production methods are involved, that expense is not prohibitive, components produced with the maximum economy of time and materials and that the finished article will function properly and withstand normal wear and tear. As a general guide to cost, most of the teachers indicated that a price range of between £1. and £2. would be acceptable, although smaller items might be somewhat less. In general terms, there was no strong preference for any particular finish or colour, but it did seem that bright colours would be more appealing to the children.

All these factors will be important in assessing both initial designs and later prototype versions and should be carefully considered in the early planning stages.

Procedure. The method of approach should be as follows:—

(a)   Design Analysis — Basic visual concept (2 or 3 dimensional) — examination of processes and materials — functional requirements — exploration and experimentation with different solutions.

(b)   Selection of Design — modification of original idea according to limitations of materials and processes selected — costing to be carried out.

(c)   Synthesis — (1) — Worksheet to be produced with information and diagrams under following column headings I. Design Project Details. II. Visualization (sketches) III. Materials & Processes IV. Conclusions.
              (2) Scale or full size working drawing to be produced.

(d)   Realisation of Design — production of final solution probably in model form.

Information. Research and reading should be carried out by all pupils taking part but staff will be available for advice on technical and other matters. Catalogues showing current manufactured products are available from your teachers on request but direct copying of ideas from these will not be permitted.

Appendix B

ORANGEFIELD BOYS' SECONDARY SCHOOL
FACTORY WEEK PROJECT

Market Research Questionnaire   Date . . . .

Name of school . . . .

Some boys at Orangefield are carrying out a design and production line project to introduce them to the methods and conditions of a manufacturing industry. Part of this involves the carrying out of market research and subsequently the design and quantity production of a simple article in the school. We should be most grateful for the co-operation of staff in our neighbouring primary schools to complete the following questionnaire and assist in this project. This in no way commits anyone to FURTHER PARTICIPATION OR PURCHASE OF THE EVENTUAL PRODUCT, unless they wish to do so, but is simply to assist us in identifying the most saleable article. Please answer all the questions and sign, in order to authenticate the return. Thank you in anticipation.

W. Comyns, B. Moffett, C. Weathers, M. Douglas.

1 Which 3 of the following would you be most likely to buy? Place in order of preference: 1, 2, 3.

Pupils' counting aids (abaci, matching cards, peg boards, etc.) ☐
Class teaching aids (clock faces, demonstration models, etc.) ☐
Manipulation toys (building, matching, threading, etc.) ☐
Shape recognition aids (simple geometric, letters, numbers, etc.) ☐
Classroom storage equipment (book racks, tidy boxes, holders, etc.) ☐
Group play aids (folding screens, work easels, sandtrays, etc.) ☐
Anything in a category not mentioned above (please specify) ☐

2 In which material/s would you prefer the article/s to be made? Please tick your preference.

(a) Mainly wood ☐   (b) Mainly metal ☐
(c) Mainly plastic ☐   (d) Mainly card ☐

3 What would you be prepared to pay for such an article? Please tick your preference.

(a) between 25p and 50p. ☐
(b) between 50p and £1.00 ☐
(c) between £1.00 and £2.00 ☐
(d) over £2.00. ☐

4 Would colour be important to you? (Please delete as necessary)
YES/NO

5 If yes, what colour would you prefer? Please tick your preference.

Blue ☐   Red ☐   Yellow ☐   Black ☐   White ☐   Green ☐   Nat. Wood ☐

6 Please indicate the specific article relating to one of the above categories *or otherwise* which would be of interest to you.

. . . .
. . . .

7 Would you be prepared to assess and assist in the final selection of the most appropriate design(s) of these products by coming to an exhibition of the students' solutions, at a later date? (Please delete as necessary)
YES/NO

Signature . . . .

Appendix C Pupils' advertising leaflets

SHOE LACER

CAN YOU AFFORD TO MISS THIS OFFER at a give away price of 30p and finished in a number of bright colours?

USES — To teach young children how to tie their laces.

It is easy to store — NO SHARP EDGES — the shoe is made of plywood.

Holes are lettered from A to H which makes it easy to be able to learn to tie their laces.

ADJUSTABLE BOOK HOLDER

This holder will be adjustable with about two to three holes so it can be made longer or shorter. The holder will also be made of wood and plastic and will have no sharp edges. This rack will hold 62 ladybird books or alternatively a lesser number of larger volumes. It comes to you at the amazingly low price of 75p.

NUMBER RECOGNITION CARDS

These number and shape recognition cards are made of brightly coloured durable plastic. They are very safe for young children as they are washable and non-toxic with no sharp edges. They can be used by teachers and children alike and if paint is available can be used as stencils. Supplied as a set of ten they are competitively priced at £1.00. Complete with storage box and instructions.

Dimensions: 100mm x 100mm.   Colours: Blue and Yellow.

Appendix D Fascimiles of share certificate and order form

ORANGEFIELD CONSTRUCTIONS LTD

This is to certify that..

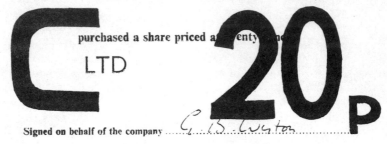

purchased a share priced a̶ ̶ ̶enty ̶

LTD

Signed on behalf of the company ......G. B. Cunton......................

Issued.................................   Redeemed................................

Share No.........

ORANGEFIELD CONSTRUCTIONS LTD.

ORDER FORM   Order No._____

ARTICLE	QUANTITY	NAME	SCHOOL	COST
Shoe Lacer				
Number Recognition Cards				
Adjustable Book Holder				
TOTAL			TOTAL	

Chapter 7

A chemical company at Ynysawdre Comprehensive School

E. T. Naughton

The original idea for the formation of a Chemical Company at Ynysawdre Comprehensive School was stimulated by the introduction of the CIA (Chemical Industries Association) Link Scheme in South Wales. This first CIA meeting was held at British Petroleum (Barry, S. Wales). Members of the university education and science departments (University College, Cardiff), industrialists and teachers were gathered to discuss the problems of the declining interest of sixth-formers especially in the field of science for industry and in the chemical industry in particular.

One of the immediate outcomes of the meeting as far as the school was concerned was the formation of a link between the school and British Petroleum (UK). The problem now was how to launch and ensure sustaining interest in the CIA Link Scheme. Should it be the usual approach, such as taking a specific piece of work or a specialist piece of apparatus and concentrate, with interested pupils, on the details of these, or encourage more industrial visits or more of the usual activities done in the past? However well many of these things had been done, perhaps they were not too appropriate for the future.

Specific problems associated with any industry would have little appeal for a large comprehensive school of about 1,500 pupils with wide-ranging abilities. Why not simulate a complete chemical industry? Include initially, with an interested group, all the decision-making and problem-solving normally encountered in the chemical industry. This should further the aims of science teaching and provide the pupils with the view that science is a reality and not teaching in a vacuum. What kind of chemical industry was the next problem. How could they carry out research, development, production, marketing, selling, etc., with limited material, equipment, space and at this stage unknown interest? The most convenient industry fitting this bill seemed to be the production of cosmetics. Opinions of members of staff, especially

103

those who were likely to be called upon for help, were sought. The opinions of the first year sixth form were also sounded out. Wholehearted approval was obtained from all people consulted and as a result the school cosmetic company was born.

Start of the project

The project was taken up by the first-year sixth form with nothing but enthusiasm and some ideas. Discussions were started with the sixth form any break-time, lunch-time and eventually for an hour or so one evening every week. At first the group were convinced that making cosmetics on a small scale was no great problem, so long as the materials were available.

They did manage to obtain some money from the then headmaster, who was about to retire. Maybe this influenced his decision! 'How much do you want for the project?' was his reaction. A figure of £100 was mentioned and after much further discussion they got £10. It was agreed at this stage to negotiate for further monies by borrowing, when necessary, from the 'school fund'. This £10 was used to buy materials for a range of cosmetic formulations.

They had a number of established formulations and their preparations, on a small scale, seemed to be the least of the group's problems.

The group thought two very important problems would be first, the difficulty of making a relatively simple material look attractive, that is, packaging, and second, what should that package contain. That is the problem of market research.

A meeting was arranged at the school with their 'link man'. The outcome of this meeting was a visit to the nearby BP factory to see the industry but more importantly to obtain the answers to two specific problems — how to solve the packaging and market research difficulties. Because of the relevant reasons for the visit this proved to be one of the most successful visits that the sixth form had been on. This comment from the sixth form may have been due not only to the excellent way in which they had been introduced by the experts to the problems of market research and packaging, but also perhaps to the excellent lunch that was provided.

This industrial link-up certainly acted as a source of encouragement and most of the sixth form returned to school with new enthusiasm for the project. Some of the market survey reports recently conducted in the UK for cosmetics had come up with results very similar to those discussed by the group whilst in school. At BP they were introduced to the idea of 'Desk Surveys' and to the idea of gaining information by the 'Gallup Poll Method'. The last method had been tried in the school magazine, but with very little success.

To get the right goods to the right place at the right time and at the right price appealed to most of the sixth-formers. What were these right goods? Where were they going to be sold? How many of them were going to be sold? What sort of profit were they going to be content with? The profits, incidentally, were to be put back into the company and go to the 'school fund'. If and when they ever sold cosmetics and made a profit what problems would these bring. Would they have to pay purchase tax? Would the local tradespeople object to this type of concern? They certainly have not got all the answers to these problems, but the response by outsiders locally has been nothing but encouraging. A local pharmacist has willingly added to their list of formulations and advised them on the problem of insurance. Contacts at the tax office inform them that providing they keep within certain limits, the work being voluntary, etc., they will not be subject to tax. Two other local business concerns have offered to sell their materials. It was decided, however, to confine sales to the school population.

Formulations for talcum powder, hand creams, shampoos were tried and evaluated. Progress was furthered by each member of the group, about ten in all, being given specific jobs of work to do. A director was elected and other positions concerning research, development, publicity, market research, etc. were also taken up by members of the group. One of the main difficulties at first was the problem of obtaining supplies from outsiders of packages, raw materials, etc. and at the prices and quantities wanted. With these difficulties not solved, the activities were curtailed with ending of the school year. Members of the then form five were also informed of their possible involvement in the following year if they stayed on in form six.

The new group

The project was restarted most enthusiastically by the next first year sixth. A large number of pupils, arts pupils as well, when given an opportunity to choose their activities chose to join the Cosmetic Company. The project has now been 'timetabled' with one hour per week and the use of the chemistry laboratory. Again, a structured arrangement was encouraged, a director was elected and others given specific areas of work to concentrate on.

There was an initial induction period for the group — going over the ground already covered by the founder members. A number of pupils in the group have shown great determination in following up the discussion work with laboratory preparation and evaluation. Many have pushed ahead despite difficulties, they have obtained encouraging contacts with firms in the cosmetic fields and packaging, and are pressing on now, determined to get a production line going. For this aim, the help of other departments and particularly any pupils with mechanical aptitudes was sought. Advertisements in the school magazine for willing hands and people to build production and processing equipment have been rewarding. The school magazine has been a very useful means of communication and the editor has allowed the use of it to keep the remainder of the school informed about company activities.

Problems which were of great concern to the company were how to launch a product so that it has the right appeal, what sort of display units should they have, where should they display their products. How about the pricing? How can they best advertise and achieve their aims? What about the 'eye appeal' of the finished product?

Industrial disputes in the coal industry delayed some of the work on the project. The work was taken up again later and with a determination to get some sort of production line going. Events have shown that the 'top of the pops' in the cosmetic selling field is talcum powder. It was decided to concentrate on producing talcum powder. This meant obtaining suitable containers, designing a suitable label, settling on an acceptable formulation and overcoming processing problems.

Processing problems

The difficulty of getting a solid material such as talcum powder to flow into a container in an acceptable way seemed at first an insurmountable problem. The group have solved this one and have reached a position of bottling at a rate of about one bottle every five seconds. A name for the cosmetic products was finally chosen. The group settled for the name 'SHÔVA' products. The word is an Indian word meaning beautiful. The first batch of talcum powder sold like 'hot cakes', and since then efforts have been made to replenish dwindling container stocks. The recently appointed secretary (like all previous secretaries) has contacted many manufacturers of packages. It seems, however, that they lose interest from a 'supply point of view' when they realise the company does not want quantities of containers of the order of 10,000 at a time.

The group realised the importance of a good package in the business of marketing a cosmetic. It was not their intention to 'bamboozle' customers with 'fancy packaging', but it is important to create the image of makers of a dependable product. The packages wanted are not only for the bottling of talcum powder but for other products which the group feel they could manufacture easily. For this purpose products such as bath salts, bubble bath and hand creams are being investigated.

Since packaging has proved more of a problem then expected, the processing of plastics has become more important than ever. Laboratory work and experiments with plastics are being carried out to get some experience of the materials. It is hoped that this will help when the group gets down to the serious business of making their own containers. The link man has helped considerably in getting started in this latter problem. The current first year sixth form science (most of the company is made up of these pupils) visited BP mainly to get an insight into problems of plastic processing and to see the type of techniques and machines used for different packages. The pupils interested in the making of 'dies' and plastic forming machines are busily 'tormenting' the members of the metalwork department to help in getting some sort of plastic-forming process going. BP have promised the company a small machine that may be used for compression moulding. If it is not possible to make a bottle, at least it is hoped they will be able to make the simple bottle top. 'Buying time' on a bottle-forming machine will then be used to get the finished package. BP have said they may 'buy time' on their machines for this purpose. If and when this happens they will visit BP again.

Planning and the future

Planning and documenting a project of this nature has been some concern for some time. Now before a branch of the project is started or an interest is being 'followed up' an attempt to crystallise the ideas, etc., are put on a 'Project Proposal Form'. They do not want the project to be a 'paper exercise', but often work is transferred from one group to another and this is done to avoid going over similar ground. A questionnaire was drawn up by a fifth-year group and presented to existing members and then used when they joined the company. This was intended to keep continuity between the succeeding sixth form groups involved in the Company.

Perfumes and their role in the cosmetic field have captured the interest of a number of the 'budding chemists' in the Company. This interest was stimulated by a film-strip on 'The Making of a Perfume' by Goya. Since steam distillation and solvent extraction form an important part of the normal Chemistry 'A' Level syllabus, it is going to be used, perhaps for once with some relevance attached to it. Information on their extraction process has now become important to the Company. Goya has given some background information in perfumes and offered to help the Company in future if they need it.

A history of the project is being kept and its value to the Company was put to the test before the Christmas holidays this year. How were they going to sell their last production run of talcum powder? This problem concerned the Company and it was decided to hold an exhibition of the Company's activities, hopes and claims to fame.

The exhibition showed the processes involved in the making of the 'talc' and showed photographs and reports about the Company. Products made on a small scale were displayed and a questionnaire on products pupils would buy was also answered by pupils present. The exhibition was set up in the Chemistry Laboratory and practically all the stocks of talcum powder were sold.

There has been interest of a more threatening kind. This time in the form of the Alkali Inspector, who, fortunately for all concerned, was satisfied that working conditions in the Company did not violate, as far as he could see, any of his rules and regulations.

Despite gloomy forecasts for the future of the Company, interest has been sustained by every new incoming sixth form. Three highly acceptable products, talc, bubble bath and after shave are being marketed at the present time. Opportunities for the sixth form to interact with the lower school and, hopefully, stimulate interest in Science occur frequently and have proved fruitful for all concerned.

Relevance and technological awareness are obvious benefits from such a project. There are many others. Decision making, and an opportunity for sixth-formers to participate and obtain an insight into the meaning of the need for creativity are amongst them. This latter need for inventiveness and creativity in the Company stimulated an interest in these subjects.

Chapter 8

Case studies in work experience at Marion High School, South Australia

B. D. Hannaford

In this study, work experience is described in both its narrow and its wider definitions. Under the more restricted definition we will be referring to cases where students are released from traditional school studies to have an experience in the work-place. However, there is an equally valid view which describes work experience as a complex of factors which join together to enhance the employability of a student. In this latter case it is not always easy to tease out the job component, because what is closely related to job preparation for one student may be general education for another student in the same group. In another sense, the whole of a general education enhances employability if the content of the syllabuses can, in any way, be shown to be useful to the student. We must never forget that liberal studies were always meant to be useful. When courses drift away from usefulness, as can easily happen in a changing world, school loses its relevance to life, including that part of it which is spent in the work-place.

Work experience for secondary school students was introduced in South Australia in 1969 in spite of some resistance from employers. It was first organized through, and with the co-operation of, local government agencies.

Now accepted by employers as a useful service, which benefits both the employers and their future employees, it is backed by agreements involving the unions as well.

Marion's policy has always been one which permitted no payment. Hence there has always been a conscious effort to balance an employer's cost against the effective productivity of the student.

Work experience has taken many forms and these are outlined in the sections which follow.

1 Work experience for full-time students

One view of our total school programme sees it as having three main components: vocational training, training for leisure, and social education. For full-time students, work experience is part of the vocational training in that total programme. This does not mean that students undertake courses, or parts of courses, labelled 'vocational', but rather that such things as skills-training, work-observation and facing up to the expectations and conditions of the work-place are aspects of their normal school programme.

Besides this, however, students may elect to take a specific course in career education.

The following are offered:

Year 11   a half-year course (72 hours)
Years 10-12   a 6-week course (24 hours)
Years 10-12   a 3-week course (12 hours)
                 holiday work experience

Students are further supported in the area of vocational training by having free access to career information and advice. These come from the Student Counsellor and the career education teacher, through printed material sent to the school and displayed on notice boards, and from representatives of various professions, trades, etc. who come to the school to address students and/or to speak to them individually at seminars arranged by such service agencies as Rotary or Kiwani Clubs or by the school.

Further to this, each student who undertakes one of the career education courses follows a programme of work observation/work experience. This consists of two contrasting three- or four-day periods of work observation or one period of work experience and one or more opportunity of contrasting work observation.

2 Work experience in a part-school, part-work programme

In this programme students gain experience of the work-place in the most direct way of all — by actually working in a part-time job. They also come part-time to school and take two or three subjects. Students of this type frequently return to full-time study because their horizons have widened and their ambitions have crystallized through what they have learnt as part-time members of the work force.

3 Work experience as part of a number of subjects

Some of the subjects of the school curriculum, by their very nature, provide opportunities for students to have work experience as they pursue the subject. These subjects are computing, materials practice and technology, food technology, food and catering, business studies and social science. In this latter subject senior students may work as tutors to younger students and even give some simple counselling or work in an institution for several hours per week, be taught the functions of the institution, its philosophy, organization and particular group of skills. In the food area the students prepare and deliver food to the school cafeteria, student camps, regular or casual dinner meetings and so on. With materials practice and technology some real assignments are included either on campus or on behalf of a nearby primary school or school for disabled children.

4 Work experience in a study-work programme (the industrial mode)

This is another programme in which young people can get experience of work by actually working. The course is offered to young people who have finished with normal schooling in years 11 and 12 and who have failed to find employment. It takes place on the school campus and can be said to follow an industrial mode because it is structured within a 35-hour week and uses the cultural environment of the work-place. The students concerned work in a genuine job situation and are released to attend classes in two subjects of their choice. Within their job areas they are supervised by qualified personnel who ensure that work is of a satisfactory standard. In addition, students receive pay for fifteen hours of productive work per week and this allows them to earn in excess of unemployment benefits. They are also treated as young adults, a practice which increases their self-esteem quite markedly.

The students are under the direct control of a manager, who supervises their work, and a Director of Studies (a teacher with industrial experience), who organizes their study programme and advises them in this area. Among the jobs available are printing, computer operation, office work, garden and grounds maintenance jobs, industrial sewing, machine maintenance work, food preparation and delivery, animal care, care of recreational and PE equipment and facilities, and factory work, which covers a variety of trades.

The factory generates most of the cash, needed to pay the manager and the students, by renovating furniture for resale, landscaping contracts and manufacture of playground and other school equipment.

5 Work experience within the school (leadership training and inside work experience)

These two kinds of work experience are carried out as part of the general 'enrichment' programme of the school. They are offered to twelfth year students as alternatives to a range of leisure-training activities such as astronomy, motor mechanics, international cookery, etc.

Those who undertake 'leadership training' go into nearby primary schools for two 1½-hour sessions a week and assist teachers in classroom work. In this way they are trained to be responsible and to work with people and are generally able to broaden their experience as young adults. The teachers with whom they work report on their performance and this report is entered on their School Leaver Statement. They also receive a certificate from our school which indicates that they have been successful in this activity.

Students who elect to do inside work experience spend the same two 1½-hour sessions working in one of the faculties, departments or work areas of the school, e.g. library, office, book-room, etc. The standards and conditions they must meet are those of the work-place. At the end of the course they are assessed on the following criteria:

quality of work	dependability
quantity of work	character
judgment	personality
willingness	appearance
industry	improvement

Those who receive satisfactory ratings for eight or more of the criteria are awarded a certificate to show to prospective employers. One unsatisfactory rating is sufficient for a student not to qualify for a certificate.

6 Work experience in holiday-time

Work experience, in the narrower sense of working for a few days actually in the work-place, covers the full range of jobs. It is sometimes convenient for students to have this experience during their holidays. While this option is available to all students, it is primarily designed for able students planning to enter the professions.

7 Work experience as part of course education

When Career Education was first offered as a subject, experience soon showed that few students were interested in the detail of the course until they had decided to look for a job. For this reason the short three-week course was introduced for those who had not opted for the longer ones.

As indicated earlier, the courses offered are:

A   Half-year course for year 11
  1   Choosing a job
  2   Source of information
  3   Interview techniques
  4   Letter of application for jobs
  5   Application forms
  6   Telephone skills
  7   World of work (classification of workers, unions)
  8   Starting a job
  9   Keeping a job
 10   Self-employment
 11   Literacy and numeracy (for entrance tests for jobs)
                            (for general survival)
 12   Banking, finance, money
 13   Consumer affairs
 14   Taxation
 15   Health and safety at work
 16   Budgeting
 17   Legal aid
 18   Community resources
 19   Unemployment
 20   FUTURE LIVING   (a)   computers
                      (b)   job changes
                      (c)   energy
                      (d)   leisure
                      (e)   cottage industries

Speakers include
Union official
Employers
C.E.S.
Bank
Legal aid

Visits
Career Reference Centre

C.E.S.
Large factory

B Enrichment Course – 7 weeks
Students participate in Outside Work Experience (one visit to an employer for three days). Course outlines include:

   (a)   Choosing a job
   (b)   Sources of information for finding a job
   (c)   Interviews
   (d)   Letters
   (e)   Application forms
   (f)   Telephone skills
   (g)   World of work
   (h)   Unions

C A three-week course for years 10-12 (six lessons per week)
This course is designed to help those students who intend leaving school very soon. It is held towards the end of each term and includes two job observation visits to employers and the course content revolves around 'job-hunting skills'.
Course content:

   (a)   Interviews
   (b)   Finding jobs
   (c)   Application forms
   (d)   Letters of application
   (e)   Telephone skills
   (f)   Literacy, numeracy (Aptitude tests)
   (g)   Unions

8 Work experience and migrant students

Taking work experience in its broadest sense as those processes by which we improve a student's employability, we see that the migrant student who has little command of English has a particular problem. For him, all the other aspects of the work experience programme will be pointless until he has acquired a reasonable facility in the language.

It is also important for the migrant student to become integrated into his new environment and to feel accepted and comfortable so that he is socially at ease when he goes to seek employment.

To these ends we have set out to provide for all our students from various ethnic backgrounds (more than forty languages, representatives of every continent have been identified) a school environment and a programme which will meet their needs.

In the first instance, there is an Ethnic Advisory Committee to handle matters concerning migrant students and their families and to arrange functions such as a one-day International Festival, meetings of parents, slide evenings, etc. We also have a senior staff member who looks after these students. He gets to know them well, is available for help and consultation when needed, and organizes and supervises their language programmes.

For many migrant students, these language programmes are of two kinds: the learning of English and the continuing study of their own language and culture.

(a) Foreign languages for English-speaking students

As in all traditional Australian high schools, the numbers of Marion High School students taking a foreign language in the first sense have fallen with the changed requirements for university entrance. We do, however, recognize that there are students with a particular bent for language study and to these we offer in the 8th year a more intensive course in French or German and then Japanese as a second foreign language later in the year. Thus we have a number of English-speaking students who go on to study two foreign languages throughout their high school course. Among these 'special' language students there will also be some whose native language is not English and who will study their own language as well. That is, this latter group will be studying four languages altogether.

(b) English for non-English-speakers

More than a quarter of Marion students were either born in one of twenty-five or more non-English speaking countries or come from families where one or both parents have come from abroad. In most of these students' homes a language other than English is the main one spoken, chiefly so that efficient communication between children and parents can be maintained.

With such a large number of the school population coming from different national backgrounds we are developing programmes which try to meet the individual needs of these students. The task is a complicated one, as we are not dealing with a homogeneous group. There are students who know hardly any English, some who are halting in the tongue and others whose English is excellent and who are also very successfully learning a third and fourth language. The problem is how to cater adequately for all of them.

In the first place we have a language Senior in charge of all the programmes and activities for ethnic students. This teacher is himself a migrant and so he has a natural understanding of the problems with which the ethnic student is faced. He is also a very kindly person who quickly gets to know his charges very well and takes a personal interest in them.

This kind of pastoral care is also extended in the multi-cultural centre at the school — a small suite of rooms where ethnic students go for English lessons given by three specially trained teachers. This area quickly becomes for them a home-base where they are sure of finding help and know that they will be understood. But it in no way becomes a ghetto, for English-speaking students visit there frequently and friendships across racial boundaries are quickly formed.

Migrant students who are 'new arrivals', and who know practically no English, at first spend approximately half their time taking special English lessons and the rest in normal classes. As their English improves, this ratio is changed until they are finally able to follow the normal school timetable. The amount of time this process takes varies with the ability and dedication of the individual student, but the motivation is strong and it is not uncommon to see them achieve this success within a year or fifteen months. The second phase of learning English, for these students, comes with expansion of their vocabulary as they work in other subjects, mix with other students and undertake a formal study of their own language which requires precise translation into and from English.

9 The place of mathematics in work experience

Again, taking work experience in its broad sense, we have realized that there is need to provide for students of middle ability mathematics courses with some appropriateness for employment. And so we have included in our curriculum the following subjects.

Year 11	Business mathematics
	Accounting
	Applied mathematics
Year 12	Business mathematics
	Applied mathematics

A broader view of work experience in which all aspects of the school's programme are seen as contributing to a student's employability

It is our belief that a young person who has known what it is to experience success, is socially at ease, has a sufficient degree of self-esteem, is equipped with necessary skills and has learned to care about other human beings, will be eminently employable. For this reason we see the total school programme as being, among other things, a preparation for the working life. It is appropriate, then, to describe the programme, even if only somewhat briefly.

1 The school culture

A school's culture can be seen as the accepted practices of day-to-day life in that school. It is in this area that the reasons lie for the rejection of school by many young people. It behoves us, as educators, then, to look at the expected behaviour patterns in our schools and to ask if they are reasonable in the 1980s or whether our students are right in rejecting them.

An examination of this area of schooling soon shows that it is dominated by myths. Much of what has been seen over many years as acceptable behaviour within our schools has come from outmoded fashions or from designs which were developed to make it possible for a teacher to cope with large numbers of students engaged in a variety of tasks.

In some schools, for instance, enormous importance is attached to the students' wearing of uniforms. Some teachers have accepted the notion that wearing a uniform is related to learning performance and yet there is not a shred of evidence to support this. Wearing a school uniform is but one aspect of our preoccupation with uniformity, an idea which is used to cover a variety of selfish decisions. And yet few schools would not include development of an individual's personality and talents among their more important aims.

Similarly, there has grown up in secondary schools a bias in favour of academic learning as opposed to technical and practical subjects. This has influenced such things as the allocation of teachers to classes, the arrangement of classes along a corridor, the packaging of subjects, and teachers' comments upon students' other achievements. All of these are ways of demonstrating a belief that academic areas of learning are superior to others. That students have rejected this myth should give us cause for rejoicing.

There are other practices, too, which are rightly resented by today's students, e.g. choosing the intellectually less able for the menial tasks about the school and the 'brightest' as leaders; insisting upon an out-moded and unnecessary set of school rules, artificial separation of teachers and students. In other words, schools create the very barriers they claim to abhor with the result that many students develop negative attitudes towards school.

At Marion High it has been our aim to create a school culture in which the students will feel comfortable, secure, accepted and stimulated, where there will be warm relationships between students and staff members who are available and accessible, and where there is equality of esteem for all learning. Standards of learning will be relevant to the age in which we live, challenging and yet attainable, and rigorously pursued. The environment will be physically attractive and all members of the school community will be socially concerned. Students will not be irked by having to abide by a set of pointless rules but will rise to the expectation that they behave in a sensible and considerate manner. The informal curriculum will provide back-up to experiences which are rich in opportunities to learn to be sensitive to people's troubles and to lend support where necessary. And the result of such a 'culture' will be a group of happy, busy young people.

2 *The curriculum*

Because one of the basic tenets of the school's philosophy is that all students should be able to be successful, we offer a very broad curriculum. All options are kept open by making a study of English, mathematics and science compulsory in the junior school years. This means that students can elect to do subjects in which they feel they have some ability and which they see as relevant. Furthermore, subjects are taught at five different levels – Advanced, Credit, Standard, Modified and Basic – where expectations and teaching methods vary according to level. Upward movement through the levels is essential, readily possible and encouraged. In this way all students are able to have a success experience, and this is reinforced by a 'rewards' system in the form of commendatory notes sent home to parents, merit certificates and certificates of achievement.

The student who is working in subjects of his choice and who is experiencing success is going to leave the school with some self-esteem and a sense of achievement. Surely, these things in themselves are part of preparation for the work-place?

Similarly, even though subjects of a more practical and/or less academic nature may not be actual training for particular jobs, they will be providing students with skills which they will be able to use in the work-place, and students will see them as having some relevance for their future.

Students choose their courses from a very wide range of subjects which cover the following areas:

Academic	Commercial
Manual crafts	Technology
Art	Physical education and sport
Music	Career education and preparation
Drama	Enrichment (leisure-time activities).

For students with particular talents, 'special', or intensive, courses are offered in:

French
German
Music
Drama
Physical education

The following special courses are also offered:

Remedial
Programme for the disinclined
Programme for brilliant students
Study-work programme for unemployed
Social-work programme for unemployed
Social-science-tutor programme
English for migrant students and continued study of their own language and culture.

All courses lead to a year 12 course.

In addition, this school offers a student opportunities to choose from among a range of short courses. Set up primarily to give a student new experiences which might enrich his leisure time, these can enhance his employability because they might have relevance to a job or simply because they make the student a more interesting person.

Overall, then, we are giving the student every encouragement to leave school with a report which covers his personal qualities, his study achievement and a record of other experiences. Collectively, we are consciously developing a many-sided person better able to enter the work world successfully.

Some outcomes and a general evaluation

Perhaps the best evaluation can be expressed in terms of the interest the school has created. Up to 800 visitors come to the school each year to seek guidance about setting up similar programmes in their own schools. The Principal spends a large part of his time in a consulting capacity and the demand is increasing. The Education Department has recognized the value of this trend and has supplied relief to make absence possible.

Set in an area of rapidly decreasing student population, the enrolment of the school is increasing. On local trends an estimate for 1981 of 425 is replaced by an enrolment of 1000 students.

An independent investigation of 'employability' of students, where the term means the fraction of leavers who got and stayed in jobs (the rest are unemployed or in further full-time study) showed that the school's ex-students were significantly better off than those from other schools. Especially so when the socio-economic index was taken into account.

When we address ourselves to what the school attempts to do by way of education of a student for a career, we are in danger, in a job shortage context, of looking too narrowly at curriculum. If, however, we accept that jobs are scarce, and in some areas scarcer than in others, that many and probably most jobs will be tedious, unrewarding and removed from the people that the firm sets out to serve, or from decision-making at any level, then our view of vocational education is almost as wide as that of education itself. If we realize that a satisfied worker is one who finds satisfaction somewhere in life, if not in the job then away from it, and that workers of all kinds are concerned to add quality to their lives as well as share in the nation's wealth, then we must be concerned to include a range of enriching experiences in his or her preparation for entry into the work place. At Marion High we take this latter view but modify it to include some immediate elements which provide some skill training with transfer value to a number of jobs in the business and trade areas, or with pre-requisite significance for entry to some further course of study. We are also keen to ensure that a student has some knowledge of conditions in a work place so that he or she is not handicapped at entry or wrongly placed through ignorance. There is bountiful evidence that we have had success in these pursuits.

Chapter 9

Work experience in Soviet and East European Schools

Nigel Grant

Work experience and labour training in the schools of the USSR and Eastern Europe have undergone so many changes over the decades that some observers have been tempted to ascribe the ups and downs to the momentary demands of the economy, or just to the rise and fall of political leaders. There is something in both of these interpretations, as we shall see, but we must beware of exaggerating the fluctuations in policy. In theory at least, there has been a continuing commitment to the principle of combining instruction with work training. Even in 1964, when the labour element in the general schools was being reduced, the Minister of Education of the RSFSR felt it necessary to insist that even if less time was being spent on it, the principle was not being rejected:[1]

> It is important to bear in mind that the fundamental principles of the Leninist idea of linking education with productive labour remain unshakeable — the secondary school was, is and will be a general educational labour polytechnical school with production training for its pupils.

Appeals to the authority of Lenin seem almost obligatory in the USSR nowadays, but in this case there is some justification: Lenin had a good deal to say about the role of work in the social and political education of the future citizen as well as in the training of the future worker. In this, of course, he was following Marx; unlike many of the social critics of the nineteenth century, Marx saw industrialisation as an opportunity. Perhaps the commoner reaction was to recoil from the whole process as basically inhuman; Ruskin's view can be taken as fairly typical of this school of thought:[2]

> It is our civilisation which has degraded the artisan by making man not a machine but something even inferior, a part of one, and above

all by the division of labour. He who passes his life making pins' heads will never have a head worth anything else.

Marx agreed about the dehumanisation and the evils of reducing the individual to his productive function in a society from which he was alienated, but he did not seek remedy in a return to the ethos of the craft workshop and the trade guild. Writing in *Capital*, he declared:[3]

> From the factory system budded, as Robert Owen has shown us in detail, the germ of the education of the future, an education that will, in the case of every child over a given age, combine productive labour with instruction and gymnastics, not only as one of the methods of adding to the efficiency of production, but also as the only method of producing fully developed human beings.

Vocational training was not to be ignored, but it was not the main objective; in Marx's view, work, 'not only a means of life, but life's prime want', was an essential part of everyone's social and intellectual development. There is no need to go into the details of his proposed scheme here; as Price has pointed out, Marx was no child psychologist, and 'his assertions were based on conditions very different from those today, when the possibility of education was being offered to a group previously denied it.'[4] The main point was the importance of work experience in helping the growing individual to perceive his role in society, to get him to see himself as having a part in it, and to emphasise the essential connection between theory and practice (another of Marx's basic philosophical tenets). It is significant that when Khrushchov proposed a greatly expanded system of polytechnical education and work practice in 1958, he concentrated his arguments on the expected social and ideological benefits rather than on job training and manpower planning, important though these undoubtedly were.

Broadly, then, there is a long-standing principle in Marxist educational thinking that future citizens should be familiarised, in theory and practice, with the basic materials, tools and processes of production, should learn their social and economic significance, should understand the connections between academic subjects and branches of production (e.g. the relevance of physics and chemistry to industry and of biology to agriculture); and, most important of all, should develop positive attitudes towards labour. Work, then, has been regarded as just as essential a component of education as literacy, numeracy or aesthetic and social education — indeed, as a fundamental part of the last.

It must be stressed that (again, in principle at least) polytechnical education is not the same thing as vocational training. According to a recent Soviet article: 'Like Marx, Lenin saw two aspects — economic and political — in polytechnical education. He was sharply opposed to the narrow training of craft workers in vocational-technical training schools.'[5] Some vocational training there had to be, and the Soviet Union during the 1920s developed an extensive network of vocational schools for the training of adolescents in skilled trades. But this kind of training was not to take over the general schools; nor was it to be the be-all and end-all even of the vocational institutes: 'Lenin noted the need to link vocational training with general and polytechnical knowledge, to avoid transforming it into narrow job or trade-training, and stressed the importance of expanding general-education subjects in all vocational-technical training schools.'[6]

This highlights the corollary of 'polytechnisation' of the general schools, often missed in the West, namely the 'humanisation' of vocational training. The argument, briefly, would go like this: pupils are future workers, and will live in a society in which work of all kinds is of fundamental importance to the 'general good; therefore work experience and labour training form an essential part of their general education. But, by the same token, one is not *only* a worker, but also a citizen and a human being; therefore some breadth has to be retained even in specifically vocational training. Courses on labour were the practical outcome of the first principle, and the inclusion of social studies, general science and literature in vocational schools (a normal procedure all over Eastern Europe)[7] of the second. One way or another, work and the other aspects of the 'many-sided development of the individual' all have to be given their due place.

Some problems in practice

So far, so good: in Marxist terms (and not only these, perhaps) the position outlined is theoretically sound; but there have always been several difficulties in translating it into practice. It has not always been possible, in the first place, to form educational policy entirely in terms of long-range social objectives; the brute facts of economics, geography and demography have a habit of asserting themselves with great urgency, and their demands may not always be compatible with the long-term aims. Thus, if there is a pressing need for (say) skilled machinists to keep a Five-Year Plan up to schedule, the demand for specific (and quick) vocational training may be overwhelming, to the detriment of the general educational aspects. Conversely, if there is a desperate need for scientists or teachers, the polytechnical aspects of the general school curriculum can be pushed into the background.

Second, social attitudes may change much more slowly than political institutions. The USSR is officially a state of workers and peasants,

123

but the expression *chornaya rabota* (literally, 'black work', the kind that gets your hands dirty) is still in common use and clearly disparaging. For all the official praises of physical labour, Soviet society at large still has a pecking-order of esteem for different occupations, with highly qualified professional jobs at the top and most kinds of manual work rather far down the scale.[8] The vocational-technical schools (PTU — *professionalno-tekhnicheskie uchilishcha*), which provide specific trade-training at fifteen *as an alternative* to staying on in the general school, have not been highly regarded, the assumption being widespread that they are used mainly by the less able. Not surprisingly, work-training in the school has suffered by association: why waste your time playing about with lathes or transplanting seedlings if you are going to finish the general school and compete for higher education entry? These attitudes have been constantly excoriated by the authorities, but they have had to reckon with their existence. As Khrushchov complained in 1958:[9]

> We still have a sharp distinction drawn between mental and manual work. . . . As a rule, boys and girls who have finished secondary school consider that the only acceptable path in life for them is to continue their education in higher schools. . . . Some of them even consider work beneath their dignity. This lordly attitude is to be found also in some families. If a boy or girl does not study well . . . and fails to get into college, the parents frighten him by saying that . . . he will have to work in a factory as a common labourer. Physical work has become a thing to frighten children with. . . . Such views are an insult to the working people of socialist society.

Nor was this only Khrushchov's well-known pungency; many years later, much the same kind of thing was still being said:[10]

> Unfortunately, there still occur instances of a remaining petty bourgeois, haughty attitude to the working man and workers' jobs. Also, for a long time, the system was not based on preparing pupils for work, on developing in them a taste for manual jobs and a correct understanding of the role of productive labour in communist construction. Some pupils do not want to go into productive work, considering it to be almost an insult. Sometimes the young person finds himself in a false position because of the lordly, disdainful attitude to labour which still exists in some families.

The same threats to the young, it seems, were still being made in the 1970s as in the 1950s.

But there are problems of attitudes — or at least of understanding — on the other side. Polytechnical education may be a relatively straightforward concept in outline, but is much more difficult to translate into curricular objectives, let alone into practice. It is doubtless laudable to seek to relate the teaching of physics and chemistry to an understanding of industrial production and to reinforce this by actual experience of work, but how exactly does one go about this without distorting the content of the subjects beyond recognition or, worse, beyond theoretical usefulness? On the other hand, just what kind of work experience will introduce the pupil to the world of work in a positive sense, without degenerating into a disconnected series of meaningless tasks, or slipping over into covert vocational training? Then, of course, there is the question of time: how much of the school week can be given over to practical work without harming the general curriculum? Is there any evidence that there is much correlation between the amount of time spent on work and the competence, let alone the attitudes, acquired? The changes in emphasis on work experience have always been accompanied by changes in the amount of time devoted to it, but the fundamental question has not, it seems, really been examined — particularly since the organisation of labour training and work practice has all too often been open to the charge that, with undue emphasis on routine tasks, it was largely a waste of time anyway. Directly vocational training has at least been more popular with its recipients, having a clear and definite end in view; it is rather more difficult to convince young people clustering round a gear-cutting tool, which most of them will never use or even see in real life, that they are doing anything useful. *De facto* vocational training, though not envisaged in the polytechnical policy, often seemed an escape from this dilemma; that way, at least, the pupils got something close to a reserve qualification, and the instructors some idea of what they were doing.

Revival and reappraisal

Polytechnical education enjoyed a brief flourishing after the Revolution, encouraged by Lenin's wife Nadezhda Krupskaya, but all but vanished without trace during Stalin's time. The Stalin era has been described, with some justice, as a dark age, but in education at least there were considerable advances — not, of course, that Stalin was an 'enlightener' in the Russian liberal tradition — quite the contrary — but he knew well enough the need for a high level of literacy and general education as well as advanced technical and higher education if the plans to industrialise the country were to have any chance of success. By the end of his rule, most Soviet children attended a comprehensive seven-year school; after the seventh class, some went on to learn a trade at a vocational or 'Labour Reserve' school, others took more advanced technical or semi-professional training (with a substantial element of general education) in the *technikumy* and other 'secondary specialised schools', and others again completed the last three classes of the general ten-year school, uncompromisingly academic in content and method.

This was obviously some distance from Lenin's polytechnical ideal, but Stalin was never the man to let principles stand in the way of what he saw as practical realities (his severe reduction of political schools and courses can be seen in the same light; he was not really concerned about what people thought, as long as they did what they were told).[11] The country needed skilled workers at various levels, fast, and the vocational schools could take care of that; and it needed trained specialists and professionals whom the ten-year school and higher education could supply. It was pre-war policy to move gradually to universal ten-year schooling (which would require some restructuring of vocational training); but the devastation of the Second World War delayed that for many years even as a long-term objective.

In 1958, Khrushchov initiated a major overhaul of the Soviet school system in his *Theses on strengthening the links of the school with life, and further improving the system of public education in the USSR.*[12] In terms of structure, it was an unremarkable but clear advance: the seven-year school was extended to eight years (compulsory) and the ten-year school to eleven. A three-way split after the eighth class was retained: trade training in PTUs (but with *some* general education) for one to three years; semi-professional training in secondary specialised schools, with enough general education to qualify for the secondary leaving examination, for about four years (or two, minus the general element, if it was taken *after* the general school); or completing the final classes in what was now styled (in full) the secondary general labour polytechnical school with production training (*srednyaya obshcheobrazovatel'naya trudovaya politekhnicheskaya shkola s proisvodstvennum obucheniem*), a mouthful which almost no one attempted; it was known as the eleven-year or secondary polytechnical school. As before, there were also part-time versions of this last category, the schools for working and rural youth, where courses could be taken by evening classes or correspondence.

There were, however, much more important changes in content and approach. In upper secondary and higher education, there was a marked shift towards part-time courses. (It was not long, indeed, before well over half the students in higher institutions were studying part-time.) Various barriers were set in the way of going straight into higher education from school; for instance, the gold medal (for straight top marks) no longer carried exemption from the entry examinations, and preference was given to part-time students, to those who had been seconded by their employing enterprises, and to those who had worked for at least two years in production. This *stazh*, or period in production, was not exactly compulsory, but carried so much weight in the selection procedure that within a year or two about 80 per cent of entrants were *stazhniki*. (The exceptions were mostly mathematicians and physicists, for whom a case for special treatment could be made.)[13]

The most striking feature, however, was the emphasis given to labour training and work practice. This began in school workshops and plots at a very simple level, but progressed to much more complex skills (such as assembling radio sets) by class VIII. For those continuing in classes IX-XI, the principle was taken further, with one-third of curricular time being spent on production practice in factories or on collective and state farms. The intention behind this was not vocational; schools made arrangements with particular factories, even if few of the pupils had the slightest intention of taking up any of the particular trades on offer, so that they would become used to the realities of working life, and acquire 'respect for work and for people who work'. As Khrushchov put it more pithily, 'Learning and labour go together' (a rhyming jingle in Russian — *Uchenie i trud vmeste idut*). It was not supposed that the new system could be introduced overnight; as so often happens in the USSR, it was expected that the reforms could be implemented right away in the major towns, but would take many years to reach the villages and remote areas.[14]

But it was not long before criticisms began to make themselves heard, and in 1964 a retrenchment was announced. Time for production practice was cut back in the senior classes from a third to a quarter of the total, the eleventh year of the general school was removed (though the eight-year basic school remained), and longer-term procedures were set in motion to develop new school programmes and to rationalise polytechnical education and production practice. The principle (as we have seen from the Minister's statement) was not rejected, but it was argued that the facilities were lacking to make it educationally effective on such a large scale:[15]

> The chief reasons (for deficiencies in production training) lie in the fact that the necessary procedure has not been introduced everywhere.... There has also been a lack of clarity in the planning of production training. ... Many programmes were needlessly overloaded with material not clearly needed ... which artificially prolonged production training and, consequently, the length of course in the secondary school. All this caused serious discontent among pupils, parents, and teachers as well.

There had been discontent also among factory managers, who were not

127

all convinced about the value of polytechnical education anyway. Few of them had the facilities for constructive work practice, and while they were quite prepared to have pupils visit their factories for the occasional 'polytechnical excursion', they did not relish having them under their feet for three half-days a week.

Two years later there was a further shift of emphasis. In a major policy statement in 1966, M.A. Prokofiev, Minister of Education of the USSR, announced a package of measures, not all of them strictly related to work training, but relevant all the same. Not only was the reduction of time for work experience confirmed, but it was substantially moved back from factories and farms to school workshops and plots. Some schools (about a third of those in the RSFSR, for instance) decided to continue with the system of external work practice, presumably because they were linked with enterprises which *did* have adequate facilities for this. Even so, Prokofiev's comment, 'Let them work out their experience', does not suggest great optimism.[16]

But other measures give a clue to the way government thinking was developing. Some of the production training had slipped, in effect, into a kind of pre-vocational training, partly because that was something that both the factories and specialist teachers knew how to do. This was replaced with a system of *vocational orientation*, 'broader than before',[17] a programme of sampling a range of jobs available in the area (without any commitment), not only to understand how they related to the local and national economy, but to help students make a more informed choice of occupation — thus serving a general educational as well as a vocational need.

At the same time, it was announced that the aim of universal ten-year schooling was reinstated, to be achieved substantially by 1970. Not everyone would necessarily go on full-time to classes IX and X, but it was made clear that this was to be the preferred route. Secondary specialised schooling (at fifteen) came next, and the PTU third, with the additional proviso that those following this path should top up their general education by taking external courses in schools for working and rural youth. A few other decisions, separately announced, are also relevant: PTU courses were to be available *after* the completion of general schooling (as secondary specialised schools already were); and in higher education, full-time courses were now preferred, and far less was heard about the *stazh* that had loomed so large in Khrushchov's time.[18]

It has already been suggested that the polytechnical principle has remained a general commitment, for political and social reasons, but that the amount of practical emphasis has varied according to the perceived social priorities and the capacity of the system (educational and industrial) to carry it. But there are other ways of making sense of the changes, which supplement rather than contradict the ideological argument, but which make more of demographic trends and manpower planning. During the Second World War, the loss of life was hideous (estimates vary from ten to thirty millions) and included a loss of birth-rate of about ten millions between 1941 and 1945. Thus, while other countries were trying to cope with the educational problems of the post-war population 'bulge', the more severe problem in the Soviet Union was a 'dent', working its way up the age-range and threatening severe manpower shortages by the late 1950s. As De Witt[19] has argued convincingly, many of the decisions of 1958 and after can be seen in this light, especially the shift to part-time courses in higher and upper secondary education. It might have been possible to pursue the goal of universal ten-year schooling and expanded full-time higher education, but only at the expense of crippling the labour-force; part-time and work-linked courses, preference to seconded students and *stazhniki*, etc., could all be argued for on social and ideological grounds − and were − but they were also the only way, at the time, whereby the expansion of the system *and* the needs of the labour force could both be maintained.

The modifications of 1964 and after also fit this interpretation. By this time, the worst of the labour shortage was passing as the 'dent' worked its way through the system, and it was possible once again to contemplate a re-emphasis on full-time study. The widely noted deficiencies and unpopularity of the massive system of work-training served to reinforce the argument. In higher education there had been problems too, including a much greater vulnerability of part-time students and *stazhniki* to drop-out; and here again a shift was possible by the late 1960s.[20] Polytechnical education, work-linked courses and work practice could now be cut back to a 'holding' position while attempts were made to rationalise and improve them, so as to realise their educational objectives without disrupting either learning or production.[21]

But a new factor had entered the calculations, one which was to re-emerge more powerfully later. It was already becoming clear that the nature of work itself was changing, that many occupations were becoming both more sophisticated and more liable to technological innovation. In the heavy industry economy of the 1940s and even the 1950s, it could still make some sense to train large numbers of adolescents for specific trades in the reasonable certainty that the skills acquired (with an adequate system of in-service training for renewal and development) would serve them for their entire working lives. Later, however, it made less sense to invest a young person's entire education in training for a job that might not exist in ten or twenty years, or one likely to change beyond recognition. Future workers would need a higher level of general *and* polytechnical education as a base on which vocational training (and recurrent retraining, as required) could be built. This could explain much of the stress on general education in the ten-year schools and the PTUs, and also the tendency to postpone specific training, hitherto an *alternative* to upper secondary education, to the post-secondary stage.

Recent developments

If the emphasis on work experience and work training had dwindled, it was not to be for long. As early as 1973, the new education law brought preparation for work forward as one of the major tasks of the Soviet school, and this was given a new prominence in the new Constitution and the 1977 Decree of the Central Committee of the Communist Party of the Soviet Union and the Council of Ministers of the USSR: 'At a time when the country is making the transition to universal secondary education, while in school, future graduates must gain a profound mastery of the basic knowledge and labour skills required to work in the national economy.'[22] Once again, the educational press abounds with articles on work-training,[23] and official and semi-official statements stress its socio-political as well as economic significance:[24]

> A highly important task of the general educational school is to increase its *social-educational function, especially with regard to the training of pupils for work in material production*. . . . The formation of a communist attitude towards labour in the production sphere is one criterion for the quality of labour education. School pupils affirm themselves as young citizens of the Land of the Soviets in social, collective labour.

The intellectual aspect — the unity of theory and practice, and the clarification of the links between scholastic knowledge and its practical application — makes its appearance too:[25]

> The drafts of the new labour-training curricula call for a significant strengthening of the polytechnic and vocational guidance orientation, for the expansion of close ties between labour training and other subjects, and for a more active involvement of the pupils in socially useful, productive labour. The draft curricula take into account the particular local features of schools in various regions and union republics.

Pupils are expected to experience work with a wide range of materials, detailed study of the latest equipment and technology, and also economics and the organisation of the various branches of production in the national economy. In the schools, the time allotted to labour training has been doubled in classes IX and X (from two hours a week to four); and outside the school, practical experience in factories and farms has been resumed. This time, however, conditions are more carefully controlled. Most regional and district departments of education have established 'inspectors of labour training and education and vocational guidance', local Soviets have appointed commissions for vocational guidance and job placement of school graduates, regional vocational guidance councils have been set up, and an All-Union Inter-Agency Council seeks to ensure co-ordination of all these activities. If the general idea is much the same as before, the organisation and control is much more elaborate.[26]

At the same time — and this accords not only with the principles enunciated by Lenin but with the needs of recurrent learning and retraining — the general educational element in vocational-technical schools has been greatly increased. 'Secondary PTUs' — that is, vocational-technical schools which also provide general education to much the same level as the upper secondary school — are by no means new. There were 146 of them in 1970, but they have been growing fast. Leningrad was the first district to go over completely to this type of PTU, but now there are over 3,600, with around two million students, well over half the entire PTU enrolment.[27] When one considers that many of the rest have already completed the ten-year school (though separate figures are not available for these), it does seem that there is a determination not only to 'generalise' vocational-technical training, for the various reasons stated, but to upgrade its standing in the eyes of the public and potential students, who have traditionally regarded the PTUs as very much a second-best academically. Whichever route pupils take after class VIII now, there is to be no opting out either from work training (of some kind) nor from general education.

But this is not simply a revised (and, they hope, more efficiently organised) version of the 'Khrushchov Reforms'; the new schemes do not place pupils in actual part-time job situations, but use formal training programmes located in schools, in production-training combines run by groups of schools, and in factories and collective and state farms. Nor is there any attempt to make the general school curriculum centre on the technical application of knowledge to work skills. The basic commitment of the curriculum is to fundamental knowledge and skills in the sciences and the humanities; polytechnical education, theoretical and practical, is an *extension* of this, not a *replacement* for it. As one recent commentary puts it:[28]

Soviet educational planners reason that *everyone* needs a basic education in language — native and foreign — literature, mathematics, biology, chemistry, physics, history and the social sciences to function productively in a highly developed society. . . . The recent quantitative expansion of compulsory education through the secondary level has been a tremendous and ambitious effort. . . . But the energies of teaching staffs and the resources of educational research have been stretched taut. The school system must now respond *qualitatively* to the needs of the enlarged senior secondary enrolment. Vocational training for some and labour training in the general-educational school make the expanded system fit national economic needs more closely.

But, once again, that is not all there is to it. The recurrent education argument looms large — significantly, at a time when by far the largest single category of post-school students (over four millions)[29] is in some form of further and adult education or job retraining. The speed of technological changes imposes this logic, even if there were no ideological argument. But it is also reinforced by demographic arguments. The birth-rate has been falling (unevenly, and especially in the more urbanised Russian areas), industrial expansion has made inroads into 'the traditional sources of incremental workers — the rural and female populations',[30] and some of the recruitment crises — albeit on a less drastic and more gradual scale — have been making themselves felt. Something had to be done to make the most effective use of potential recruits to the labour force; and the recent measures, designed to produce a broader-based vocational training *and* a more 'work-oriented' general education, can be seen as an attempt to deal with this.

Eastern Europe

So far, we have been looking exclusively at the USSR — reasonably enough, as it has had the longest experience of trying to translate Marxist-Leninist theory into practice. Also, as the dominant member of the Eastern bloc, it has been a pace-setter in this as in most matters since the Second World War. But the other East European systems, under Soviet influence though they may be, are not simply the Soviet system 'writ small'. They all have their own histories and traditions that have been adapted to, rather than replaced by, communist policy, and all have their own economic, demographic and social problems that have to be taken into account in the running of their systems.[31] On the whole, the fortunes of polytechnical education and work practice in the East European schools have reflected developments in the Soviet Union; but these reflections have not always been exact, and some have departed widely from the general pattern.

Czechoslovakia and Bulgaria have followed the various fluctuations so closely that little separate mention is necessary in a survey such as this. Poland (unsurprisingly) has not; even in the 1960s, external work practice, compulsory in many other countries, was actually illegal. Interestingly, one of the main points of the Polish education law of 1979 was a much greater stress on work experience, but that was rescinded in 1980 after the upheavals that led to the creation of Solidarity, for reasons that had little to do with work training.[32] Romania goes its own way most of the time (as, less conspicuously, does Hungary); there, the development of work-based education has usually been more directly vocational, as witness the creation of professionally oriented *specialised lycées*, rather like the Soviet secondary specialised schools (or their equivalents elsewhere) in 1966, or the opening of technical training schools for secondary school graduates, partly to take some of the pressure off higher education, partly to improve the quality of the skilled work-force.[33]

More surprisingly, it has been East Germany, usually thought of as one of the most orthodox members of the bloc, that has departed furthest from Soviet practice; but it has done so by displaying a degree of commitment and consistency through all the vacillations in the USSR. When the time for polytechnical education was cut in Soviet schools, it was *increased* in East Germany; when labour practice in factories and farms was being soft-pedalled in the Soviet system, the East Germans were giving it more emphasis, and making even more of the moral and social arguments.[34] All children in the GDR now attend the Ten-Class General Educational Polytechnical Secondary School (*Zehnklassige allgemeinbildende polytechnische Oberschule*, variously contracted to ZAPO or POS) from the age of six to sixteen. As the name implies, work training and practice figure prominently alongside the academic subjects. But there are also elaborately organised spells of practice in *polytechnical centres*, based on local factories, in which pupils have both formal instruction and experience of all the basic processes. (In a factory making washing machines, for instance, there is a complete assembly line in the centre, and care is taken that pupils change round at set intervals and sequence to experience *all* the relevant tasks, and that the significance of each is taught during the formal sessions.[35]) Beyond the tenth class there is the usual three-way divide: pupils can go on to trade training (with an element of general education) in a vocational school (*Berufsschule*), skilled trade training plus general education to the level of the upper secondary school in *Berufsschulen mit Abitur*,[36] or more academic courses in the *prolonged secondary school* (*erweiterte Oberschule* or EOS), a two-year course designed mainly for potential higher education entrants, but still with a strong polytechnical element. The general principles, then, are not too different from those outlined in the USSR; the main differences are in the much more careful organisation, and the constantly strong emphasis that has been placed on this aspect of education for decades.

One possible explanation (often produced) is the higher status accorded to skilled work in a highly industrialised society which also has a long craft tradition. It is possible that the attitudes summed up in the phrase, 'Ich bin Facharbeiter — wer ist mehr?' ('I'm a skilled worker — who is more?') are more widespread than in many other countries in the bloc. It is also true that the authorities in the GDR push every aspect of ideology more strenuously than those of other communist countries; even the Russians are inclined to say that the East Germans are 'always 120% anyway'. It could be that the native communist tradition is stronger in East Germany (Marx was a German, after all, and the Communist Party was one of the strongest parties in Germany before the Nazi take-over), but there is another possible explanation. In all the communist countries, the authorities make constant appeals to 'socialist patriotism', a frequently effective way of harnessing nationalist sentiments in an area where they usually run high. But this political prop is not available to the East German regime; most of their neighbours would be understandably uneasy about a revival of German nationalism, and in any case the great majority of Germans are across the frontier in West Germany — appeals to patriotism could undermine the very foundations of the state. Instead, ideological rectitude is pressed into service, and work training is a prominent part of that. Finally, there is the manpower-demographic argument. East Germany has suffered from a continual shortage of skilled manpower — partly because of the flood of refugees to the West before the Wall was built (and the trickle since), partly because of the declining birth-rate. Factors which have induced the USSR to point up labour training from time to time have always been there in the GDR; that *one* effect of all these factors should be a consistently prominent role for polytechnical education is hardly surprising.

More surprising, perhaps, have been recent developments in Yugoslavia, which has not been a member of the bloc since 1948 and therefore has hardly been under Soviet tutelage. The same rationale could be argued in Yugoslavia as elsewhere in Eastern Europe, of course, as it has always claimed to be interpreting Marxism in its own way. Some of the familiar features are there; in the eight-year basic school (*osnovna škola*), polytechnical education accounts for one hour per week in class V, and two in classes VI-VIII. There is a strong vocational sector — trade schools and secondary technical schools, not unlike the Soviet PTUs and *tekhnikumy* respectively both in their levels of vocational work and the prominent elements of general education. But in the *gimnazija*, the four-year general upper secondary school, two hours per week of 'technical education' has for decades been all the commitment to work training.[37] But in 1974, the Tenth Congress of the Yugoslav League of Communists resolved, among other things, that the educational system should[38]

> train young people and adults for work and encourage in them a creative attitude to work; adjust the content, organisation and method of educational activity to the needs of man and work, the development of socialist self-management relationships and the modern achievements of culture, science and technology.

In a detailed fifteen-point plan for reform of the system, including a great deal about social equality, there is provision for 'a balanced programme, strengthening ties with the whole field of work, promoting general and polytechnical education, and a Marxist ideological orientation and the ideas of brotherhood, unity and internationalism.'[39]

As elsewhere, then, we find the principle spelled out and given ideological justification. The practical implications (being pursued at different rates in the six Republics, for Yugoslavia has a decentralised system)[40] involve further unification of the school after age fifteen, in the form of a school centre (*školski centar*) offering a two-year course of general and polytechnical education and, in some cases, preliminary vocational training as well. Thereafter, in place of the discrete entities of upper secondary and higher education, what is envisaged is a series of two-year stages, up to university post-graduate level, designed to be accessible to re-entry from work at any point. Of all the options available, going straight through secondary and higher education, with no interruption for work, is the one least likely to be encouraged.

Apart from the more directly vocational nature of the programme, there are one or two other features that make the Yugoslav case unusual, Yugoslavia does not suffer from a manpower shortage; on the contrary, it is the only communist country to admit the existence of unemployment (which is getting worse, and would be worse still but for the thousands of Yugoslavs going abroad to work, especially in West Germany); but it does have a serious lack of skilled workers. Ironically, the post-war expansionist policy of opening up secondary and higher education has created problems in its success; there has long been severe pressure on academic secondary and higher education courses, to which the authorities have usually responded by more expansion. But this has been done at the expense of vocational training, creating an imbalance in the labour-force — given the present state of the economy, there are too many graduate engineers, not enough technicians and skilled workers. Like East Germany, Yugoslavia is trying to discourage professional parents from using the school system to promote their own children, while trying to encourage more able youngsters to go into skilled work. Thus, it is hoped, the 'class-tinged dualism' can be reduced, and the tendency of social class differences actually to widen can be reversed. Once again, we see work education as an attempt to change social trends. The particular problem for Yugoslavia — apart from an acute form of the usual one of translating theory into definite policy, let alone practice — is the presence of major unemployment. It is not easy to insist on alternating instruction with work if work is in short supply.

Conclusion

From an examination of trends in the USSR (and a necessarily brief glance elsewhere in Eastern Europe), it emerges that work experience is given largely social and ideological justifications, and secondarily related to the needs of the economy — more efficient work-skills, broader-based training, and so forth. The latter argument can be more compelling (and the results easier to judge), but carries the problem of keeping in mind the distinction between polytechnical education and vocational training — a theoretically important distinction, but one easily lost sight of.

But emphasis on work education, and the forms it takes, vary from place to place and time to time according to other factors, such as the needs of manpower planning and the fluctuations in the numbers of pupils and potential workers. Less obviously, social trends create their demands also, hence the attempts to discourage the formation of professional and academic elites by manipulating the system. Thus, polytechnical education emerges as a central concept in Marxist pedagogy, a contribution to manpower planning *and* a tool for social engineering — a formidable task by any standards. Further, it has taken on another role as well, namely that of providing an educational basis for lifelong learning and job retraining in a fast-changing and uncertain future.

It is hardly surprising that the outcome in any of these aims has, so far, been mixed, especially since faulty planning and disorganised execution have been common. We have already seen something of the reappraisals and revisions, as the immediate needs change and the conflicting pressures build up. It is noteworthy, however, that though there has been much searching criticism of policy and method, the assumption is virtually universal that if they can get the planning and organisation right, the rest will follow. The assumption that these tasks are possible, that society can be changed, and that education and work are inextricably linked in this, arises from a view of the nature of humankind as well as from events, and is not seriously challenged. The fluctuations will doubtless continue over the years, and the failures will emerge and be deplored, but the general policy is likely to be a continuing theme for the foreseeable future, unless the nature of work and society changes so drastically that all the assumptions on which the authorities proceed have to be re-examined and perhaps abandoned.

Notes

1 E.I. Afanasenko, 'Novyi uchebnyi god: kakim on budet v shkole?' *Sovietskaya Rossiya*, 13 August 1964.
2 J. Ruskin, *A Crown of Wild Olive*, 1886. Cited in P.W. Musgrave, *Sociology, History and Education*, London, Methuen, 1970.
3 K. Marx, *Capital*, vol. 1, ch. XV, sect. 9.
4 R.F. Price, 'Labour and education in Russia and China', *Comparative Education*, vol. 10, no. 1, March 1974.
5 N.I. Dumchenko, 'Realizatsiya leninskikh idei professionalno-tekhnicheskogo obrazovaniya', *Sovietskaya pedagogika*, 1980, no. 4, pp. 41-4.
6 Ibid.
7 See, for a background discussion, N. Grant, *Society, Schools and Progress in Eastern Europe*, London, Pergamon, 1969.
8 Joseph Zajda, *Education in the USSR*, London, Pergamon, 1980, ch. 4, sect. 1, pp. 181-201.
9 N.S. Khrushchov, *Strengthening the Ties of the School with Life and Further Developing the System of Public Education*. Theses of the Central Committee of the Communist Party of the Soviet Union and the Council of Ministers of the USSR, November 1958, sect. 20. (Published in English as *Bringing the Soviet Schools Still Closer to Life*, Soviet Booklet, no. 44, London, December 1958.)
10 N. Dyachenko, *Professional'naya orientatsiya*, Moscow 1971, p. 117, cited in Zajda, op. cit., p. 193.
11 E.P. Mickiewicz, *Soviet Political Schools: the Communist Party Adult Education System*, Yale University Press, 1967.
12 N.S. Khrushchov, op. cit.
13 Some were musicians and artists. For a discussion of educational 'special cases', see John Dunstan, *Paths to Excellence and the Soviet School*, London, NFER, 1977.
14 The widely-used escape-phrase, *v osnovnom* (basically, essentially), is usually understood to mean 'in the cities more or less right away, in the countryside when we can'.
15 'Desyatiletnyaya, Trudovaya, politekhnicheskaya', *Uchitel'skaya gazeta*, 15 August 1964.
16 M.A. Prokofiev, 'K novomu pod'emu sovietskoi shkoly', *Uchitel'skaya gazeta*, 26 November 1966.

17 Ibid.
18 For an analysis, see N. Grant, 'The USSR', in Margaret Scotford-Archer (ed.), *Students, Universities and Society*, London, Heinemann, 1972, ch. 4, pp. 80-102.
19 Nicholas De Witt, 'Polytechnical education and the Soviet school reform', *Harvard Educational Review*, vol. 30, 1960; De Witt, *Education and Professional Employment in the USSR*, Washington DC, 1961.
20 See note 18.
21 E.g. K. Ivanovich, D. Epstein, 'Znaniya, politekhnizm, trud', *Uchitel'skaya gazeta*, 20 May 1967; A.V. Kiselev, 'O syyazi tekhnicheskogo truda s drugimi predmetami', *Shkola i proizvodstvo*, 1973, no. 10; I.G. Tkachenko, 'O trudovom vospitanie sel'skikh shkol'nikov', *Shkola i proizvodstvo*, 1973, no. 12.
22 F.G. Panachin, 'Shkol'naya politika partii v deistvii', *Sovietskaya pedagogika*, 1979, no. 12, pp. 3-9.
23 E.g. M.A. Prokofiev, 'Novyi etap v razvitii prosveshcheniya', *Sovietskaya pedagogika*, 1981, no. 3, pp. 4-10; P.R. Atutov, I.D. Zverev, 'Sovremennye problemy politekhnicheskogo obrazovaniya uchashchikhsya', in ibid., pp. 11-18.
    'Podgotovku shkol'nikov k obshchestvenno poleznomu trudi i vyboru professii – na kachestvenno novyi uroven', *Sovietskaya pedagogika*, 1981, no. 6, pp. 1-9; F. Guseinov, 'Gotovym budushchikh rabochikh', *Narodnoe obrazovanie*, 1981, no. 6, pp. 56-7; L. Ignatov, 'V trude i dlya truda', *Narodnoe obrazovanie*, 1981, no. 3, pp. 60-2; L. Shilo, 'Trudovoe vospitanie – delo vsenarodnoe', *Narodnoe obrazovanie*, 1980, no. 9, pp. 71-4.
24 Panachin, loc. cit.
25 Ibid.
26 Ibid.
27 Dumchenko, loc. cit.
28 B.B. Stretch, 'Current priorities of Soviet school development', *Soviet Education*, March 1981, vol. XXIII, no. 5.
29 *Narodnoe khozyaistvo SSSR v 1979 godu: statisticheskii ezhegodnik*, Moscow, 1980.
30 Stretch, loc. cit.
31 N. Grant, *Society, Schools and Progress in Eastern Europe*, London, Pergamon, 1969.
32 The law was unpopular (especially with professional parents) because it was going to make the academic route through the *lyceum* (the upper secondary general school) more difficult; it was this, rather than work-training as such, that led to pressure for its repeal.
33 Romania's action in founding the specialist lycées actually brought it into line with the USSR and the other East European countries; but that was not (in view of political relations) the way it was put.
34 E.g. E. Kohn and F. Postler, *Polytechnical Education in the German Democratic Republic*, Ministry of Education of the GDR, Berlin,

1976; Arthur Hearnden, *Education in the Two Germanies*, Oxford, Blackwell, 1974; D. Waterkamp, *Lehplanreform in der DDR*, Schroedel, Hanover, 1975.

35 Personal visits and discussions in the GDR, February, 1978.

36 *Abitur* — the final secondary school examination in Germany (East and West).

37 Mihajlo Juhas, *Education and its Reform in Yugoslavia*, Institute for Studies in Education, Belgrade, 1975.

38 *The Tasks of the League of Communists of Yugoslavia in the Socialist Transformation of Education along Self-Management Lines*, N.p., n.d.

39 Juhas, op. cit.

40 Broad guidelines are determined at Federal level, but the bulk of responsibility rests with the six Republics and their subdivisions. The more affluent Republics, like Croatia and Slovenia, are usually years ahead of Serbia, Bosnia or Macedonia; the development of school centres has been a case in point. (E.g. *Osnove nastavnog plana i programa za srednjoškolsko obrazovanje u SR Hrvatskoj*. Zavod za unapredjivanje stručnog obrazovanja ST Hrvatske. Školska Knjiga, Zagreb, 1976.)

Index

Page numbers in bold type refer to a listed reference to an author

142